Pokemon
& Harry Potter

Dedicated to the Children

For Philip, whose quest for adventure has driven me to scour the landscape ahead for obstacles . . .

For Lindsey, whose boundless curiosity has provoked me to seek the knowledge of the Father . . .

For Brittany, whose joy unspeakable has shed constant light in the shadows . . .

For Ethan, the first born of my first born . . .

And for His precious ones everywhere, whose futures are worth our most diligent vigilance and our most focused labors . . .

Psalms 71:17-18

"... O God, thou hast taught me from my youth: and hitherto have I declared thy wondrous works.

Now also when I am old and greyheaded, O God, forsake me not; until I have shewed thy strength unto this generation, and thy power to every one that is to come..."

Table of Contents

Introduction

For nearly three decades it has been both my greatest joy and greatest heartache to minister to young people. The greatest joy has come from watching God intervene in so many young lives, often saving their lives and witnessing the redeeming power of God fill their searching hearts with the love of Christ. The greatest heartache is that there are so many yet unreached whose lives are being ravaged by the powers of darkness.

The rebellious nature of the human heart is deeply ingrained in every human at birth. From the moment we enter into this world the forces of darkness begin their conspiratorial assault upon each of us. However, not since the beginning of history have these forces of evil had available to them so many avenues by which they could carry out their diabolical plan to "kill, steal, and destroy" (John 10:10).

At younger and younger ages our society's children are exposed to the heinous, corrupt, and darker side of human depravity. A large part of this is due to the technological advances of the age. Graphic computers, television, video games, and unlimited access to the Internet have opened, quite literally, a whole new world to our youth and children. When combining our children's accessibility to these outlets with the aggressive marketing expertise of the producers of children's television, movies, and video games, it is simple to understand why Satan would focus such tremendous energies in the development of philosophies projected through these mediums.

Tragically, today the vast majority of children's television programs, video imagery, games, and animated movies and cartoons are inundated with New Age occultic symbolism and humanistic philosophies. Masquerading as innocent entertainment, the enemy of Truth has brilliantly hidden his message in a seemingly harmless shroud of fun-filled games and stories that attract our children as light attracts the moth.

Uninformed and unsuspecting parents are not only being deceived by this ploy but are, in fact, facilitating the brainwashing and demonic indoctrination of their own children.

Some may feel that such talk is an overreaction to what they consider harmless children's entertainment. Perhaps as they read these pages their eyes will be opened and they will be able to see through the diabolical camouflage of the satanic agenda.

You may ask, "Are you implying that our children are full of demons?" Not necessarily.

What I am saying is that part of our conscious, decision-making mechanism that ultimately determines our actions is the true focus of all satanic efforts. If he can teach us at an early age to think incorrectly about evil, about God, and about biblical truth, then he can easily succeed in getting us to live incorrectly.

It is of paramount importance parents realize that, knowingly or unknowingly, they, as well as their children, are involved in a great universal spiritual battle. From our earliest years each of us have been exposed to the "spiritual wickedness in high places" (Eph. 6:12). Forces that we cannot see are hard at work attempting to influence our decision-making processes with evil suggestions.

God's Word instructs Christians how to discern the difference between the voice, intent, and influences of God versus those of the Devil. Christian parents are instructed to know what influences are beneficial to the spiritual health, well being, and development of their children. Conversely, parents should be able to recognize the influences of the Evil One and to protect their children from his lying and seductive assaults upon sensitive young minds and hearts.

Parents who value the lives and care about the eternal destination of their children cannot play the role of the proverbial ostrich with his head buried deep in the sand. The reality of profound danger to their child's future exists whether they acknowledge it or not.

You may respond by stating that your child is a Christian and that as Christians we are protected from demonic assault. However, that is not biblically sound doctrine. The enemy is aiming his most powerful weapons at the Christian home and especially at Christian children.

Christian parents must be more vigilant now than ever to insure that they teach their children the spiritual nature of the world in which they live. The subtle, and not so subtle, influences of the New Age, witchcraft, and the occult are everywhere as Satan is working overtime to seduce this generation.

God's Word gives us definitive spiritual strategies for recognizing, fighting, and winning every spiritual conflict we encounter. But parents must aggressively work to know how Satan is assaulting their children and then take the proper remedial steps to protect and shield them from these satanic schemes.

My prayer is that this book will expose the "Father of Lies" and his devious efforts to seduce our children, and that parents everywhere will discover how to win the war that evil is waging in its attempt to destroy the lives of children around the world.

A Personal Experience

Discovering Pokemon

It was a Saturday morning. I must admit that though I am usually an early riser, I am not what one would consider a "morning person." You know the type. Morning people can be most irritating to non-morning people. My lovely wife is, without a doubt, one of those folks who wakes up with a song in her heart, a skip in her walk, and just cannot wait to take on the day. I, on the other hand, need time in the morning to get my motor running. And then it takes me a couple of cups of coffee to get in gear. I have always been convinced that God must have a wonderful sense of humor to put a morning person in a marriage with a non-morning person. Such couples do indeed get numerous opportunities to draw upon the graces of patience and understanding. In fact, with every new sunrise they are afforded yet another opportunity to learn how to dwell with each other according to knowledge (1 Pet. 3:7).

On this particular pre-dawn Saturday morning, as the sun struggled to crest the horizon, I staggered into the kitchen and groped for a cup to pour some coffee. Most non-morning people, myself included, have worked out a deal with their body and sensatory capabilities. We have developed the uncanny ability to allow most of our senses to continue to sleep while using the minimum amount of conscious effort to get through the time needed to rouse ourselves into a fully awakened state. For instance, in my case, my eyes have reached a compromise where one of them can remain shut while the other opens enough to negotiate a path to the coffeepot.

As I proceeded through this morning ritual using as few of my faculties as possible, I heard the sounds of the television coming from the living room. Since it was not too far out of the way from my usual track back into my bedroom, I decided to investigate who would be up so early on a Saturday morning watching television.

Staggering into the general area of our living room with my morning gerbil-hair appearance and a steaming cup of coffee in hand, I saw my nine-year-old son sitting in front of the television. He was so engrossed in whatever it was he was viewing that he failed to notice that I was in the room.

I should point out that my wife and I have been vigilant over the years in our efforts to know what our children view on television and in movies. Not only have we screened the programming that they are exposed to but we have made great efforts to teach them how to discern the messages being promoted by the programs, movies, music, and cartoons they view. In fact, the ultimate purpose of this book is to assist parents and grandparents in developing godly appetites in the lives of their own children and grandchildren.

As I stood there in a semi-coma watching my son on that early Saturday morning view the television, I could not help but notice how "into" the program he was.

Finally I asked, "Son, what is it that you're watching?" A bit startled at my presence, he said, "Oh, hi Dad. I'm watching Pokemon."

Having never heard of Pokemon, and being only half alive to the world, I simply shrugged and turned to go back to a dark room, nurse my coffee, and attempt to slowly shake myself into full consciousness.

As I sat in my chair next to the bed I tried to think out the implication of the name of the cartoon my son was watching. I had thought he said the program was about a "pokey man." I thought that a strange title, though I did remember our children used to read a little storybook entitled *The Pokey Little Puppy*. I thought the cartoon must be about a slow-moving man like myself in the morning. Maybe it had a similar story line as the puppy book. How wrong I was.

Later that same morning, when at last I had both eyes open I asked my son, "So, how was your cartoon, and by the way, what's the story on 'Pokey Man?'"

He laughed at my mispronunciation of the cartoon and set me straight by saying, "Dad, it's not 'Pokey Man', it's Pokemon!"

So, I asked, "All right, Son, what's a Pokemon?"

His response was at best ambiguous and all he could tell me was that the cartoon was about a guy who goes around trying to catch little critters called Pokemon. Realizing the futility of probing the boy further, I decided to look into this new thing called "Pokemon" whenever I could find time to do so.

Don't get me wrong. I am not interested in such children's programs for my own entertainment and edification. However, my wife and I had learned long ago to check out anything and everything that stimulates the interest of our children. Ignoring what our children are listening to, watching, and using for entertainment can have devastating effects upon their lives and the home.

A few days later I came home and called my son into the room to sit down and talk to me. I had begun to discover some rather chilling facts about what had become not only his favorite cartoon but the favorite preoccupation of increasing millions of children across the nation and around the world.

In fact, I soon found out that Pokemon is far more than a cartoon. Pokemon is the trademark of a vast range of television productions, video games, trading cards, movies, and an ever-increasing line of Pokemon products. However, the far-reaching tentacles of the Pokemon empire should not be the primary concern of Christian parents. The overwhelming concern is the message that Pokemon is teaching our children to act upon.

Pokemon Unveiled

Many parents have placed an enormous amount of confidence in the character, integrity, and moral stability of those who are creating, producing, and marketing children's entertainment, products, toys, and programming. Naiveté, combined with the fact that parents, some single and others married, are preoccupied with making a living in a very demanding and vibrant economy, greatly hampers their involvement in their children's activities. However, the fact we cannot ignore is that the creators of the vast majority of products and programming aimed at America's children do have an agenda.

Obviously, one great motivating factor in the creation, production, and distribution of Pokemon products is money. The Pokemon cartoon series, movies, and game items are, in fact, at the last report a six billion dollar industry worldwide. Nothing is inherently evil about money, yet God is greatly concerned over the means used to gain money.

However, there can be no doubt about the fact that there are additional motives and purposes behind the massive worldwide effort to promote and market the Pokemon philosophy that so clearly permeates their product line. It would be extremely difficult to believe that the New Age, occultic, and paranormal nature of the Pokemon game, its plot, and its characters did not emanate from the deeply held belief system of some personalities at the very core of the Pokemon industrial complex. To understand this, we must take a look at the spiritual philosophy that is woven into the Pokemon video games, television series, and movies. Additionally, we must look at the goals of the main Pokemon characters and the means by which they have chosen to reach those goals. Finally, in order to grasp the potential danger of this philosophy to a young child's development we must look closely at the values, life-styles, and spiritual concepts being promoted and encouraged by Pokemon.

Friendly Monsters

As I sat down with my nine-year-old son to discuss the cartoon series he so enjoyed, the first question I asked him was, "Do you know what Pokemon means, Son?"

He thought for a minute and then confessed that all he really knew the word meant was that it was what the little creatures in the series were called.

I then said, "Well, Son, upon looking into what Pokemon is all about, the first thing I discovered is that Pokemon is short for 'Pocket Monsters.'"

My son then responded as most nine-year-olds would by saying, "Aw, Dad, that can't be true! I've not seen any monsters on the show."

The truth is very few children these days are fond of monsters in the traditional sense. But the fact is, Satan is very clever and he has succeeded in creating a world for children in which we find not only bad monsters but also good monsters.

Who can forget growing up with Casper, the friendly ghost? However, such re-characterization of an entity normally considered something evil, such as a ghost, into an entity that is something friendly, cuddly, and warm gives a psychological premise from which Satan can work.

One of the fundamental doctrines of Satanism is that evil is only an extension of good. The Satanists believe that good is actually evil and that evil is good and that both are merely a matter of subjective perception. That concept is, of course, diametrically opposed to what the Scriptures teach.

Hence, if the promoters of an occultic agenda can get their

foot in the ideological door by convincing children and their parents that sometimes evil is good and that there is nothing wrong with trafficking in occultic activity, then half their battle for the mind of that child is won.

"Certainly," you say, "nothing can really be wrong with allowing children to pretend that there are bad monsters and good monsters and good witches and bad witches." The problem with children, however, and unfortunately with many adults, is that they have not yet developed the capacity to distinguish the real from the make-believe and often cannot tell where the line between fantasy and reality is drawn.

These, of course, are only the surface issues with Pokemon. A closer look reveals the horrid truth that Pokemon is yet another effort by malevolent forces to modify the behavior of our children.

A Spiritual World

The best way to instruct children on how to learn to think critically is to first provide them with a fundamental knowledge that they live in a spiritual world. They must learn that everything in this natural world emanates from and is a reflection of the spiritual world. This is what the Word of God teaches. The Bible tells us, ". . . things which are seen were not made of things which do appear" (Heb. 11:3).

As children are taught from an early age that there is a holy, loving, benevolent God and an evil, deceptive counterpart called the Devil, a foundation is built from which a parent can relate to the child the biblical methods for discovering the characteristics of each.

As I sat discussing Pokemon that day with my nine-year-old son, I drew him into the conversation by questioning him about the nature of the characters in his favorite cartoon series.

Children are bright when presented with the basic facts.

Neither parents nor children need to be theologians. Knowing simple Bible truths and the fundamental facts are enough for children to begin to deduce the spiritual temperament of what they are seeing. If they know **truth** they, with a bit of insightful help from a committed parent, will have no problem recognizing the lie.

As I talked to my son I wanted to lead him to ultimately make the right decision on his own. He, as many children often will, had already demonstrated his ability to make the right choices on previous occasions.

Early Revelations

A couple of years prior to our Pokemon discussions, I had just returned from preaching a series of Bible conferences around the country.

While at the conference, I became acquainted with a dynamic evangelist named David Benoit. David gave me two of his powerful books, entitled *Who's Watching the Playpen?* and *Fourteen Things Witches Parents Hope Never Find Out.*

As I sat down with my son to catch up with what he had been doing in my absence of several days, the two books I had set on the end table caught the attention of my son.

He said, "Hey, Dad, can I look at these books?"

Knowing he was already a good reader but thinking he would get bored with them after a few minutes anyway, I said, "Sure, Son, go ahead."

As we sat there, he grew quiet as I relaxed watching a football game. After about forty minutes of being deeply engrossed in the books about how the occult has invaded homes through a vast number of children's videos, games, and toys, he jumped up from the couch and ran upstairs.

I, of course, thought the boy must be tired of reading and went to play. However, a few minutes later I heard a "thump, thump, thump" on the stairway. I looked around in time to see Philip reach the bottom of the staircase dragging an enormous, giant-size, heavy-duty garbage bag.

I watched the boy drag the enormous bag over to me where he said, "Dad, all these old books and videos are of the Devil!"

At first I thought, "Well, the boy's enthusiasm over what he read in the book has runaway with him." But, as he opened the bag and began to go through its contents, I was amazed at his find. Even though my wife and I had thought we had been very vigilant to protect our children from children's toys, games, and videos laced with occultic influences, it was obvious that we had overlooked much.

As Philip dumped his bag at my feet and began to go through his stash of tainted material, I took a closer look at the two books that had stimulated his housecleaning. Indeed, the boy was right. As we progress through the coming chapters, I feel many parents will have their eyes opened to the shocking number of children's products filling our homes that are inundated with dark, occultic philosophies to which few parents want their children exposed.

After going through each of the items in his bag and pointing out the problems, he then rebagged it all and dragged it out to the garbage dump.

Rarely have I been so proud of a child. He was responding quickly and with sensitivity as do most Christian children who are exposed to proper teaching.

This episode was still heavy on my mind as I began to point out some of the profound philosophical and spiritual problems that were clearly evident in his new, favorite cartoon series. However, I still did not want to mandatorily demand that he cease watching the morning program. I decided to take a calculated risk knowing he understood the premise of how satanic influences can be hidden in a plot or story, that with enough facts, he would eventually make the right choice about Pokemon.

The next couple of weeks were filled with some real challenges and surprises as we both discovered more and more about the *magical* world of Pokemon.

Was it just a game, a movie, and a cartoon? What was hidden in this Pandora's box?

Chapter 2

What Is Pokemon?

At about the same time that I began to look into the facts about Pokemon to present to my nine-year-old son, letters from our television viewers began to come in from around the country.

Here is one of those letters . . .

> . . . We are getting very worried. Some time ago our two boys, aged seven and nine, began to get into this new cartoon and game called Pokemon. At first we thought nothing of it, but now our sons have changed. I told my husband I was scared, but he laughed it off. He's not laughing anymore. They have gotten out of hand. Something is going on. Can you please advise us? . . .
> — Signed, Desperate in Houston, Texas.

While many parents may not be extremely familiar with the invasive nature of occultic and New Age influences through contemporary children's entertainment, most of them are in tune with their children's mood and behavioral swings.

The parents who penned that letter, and multitudes like them, are attesting to bizarre changes in the attitudes of children who are plunging into the world of Pokemon.

But why and how could these products so radically influence the personality and behavior of a child?

First, allow me to provide you with an abbreviated answer to the question, "What is Pokemon?"

According to information compiled from a number of websites, Pokemon, short for *pocket monsters* is an RPG/simulation Game Boy game released in 1995 by Nintendo of Japan.

Pokemon are the powerful, little monsters in the game who live, according to the game's creators, in the wild. They can be captured or conquered by the players of the game and then trained to use their powers to defend their masters, help capture other Pokemon, and/or to manifest their powers through their masters. Participants in the Game Boy game are matched against the skills of a ten-year-old boy named Ash whose goal in life is to become the greatest Pokemon trainer in the world which, of course, becomes the goal of all game participants.

In order to achieve this goal, players must encounter and fight all one hundred and fifty-plus, existing Pokemon creatures and fill up what is called their "Pokedex", or Pokemon index. To accomplish this, one must first capture a few of the monsters, train them, and get them to fight *for* you rather than *against* you.

Together, the player and his trained monsters must then fight eight Pokemon Training Hall Leaders in order to win their badges. Doing this demonstrates the player's psychic and supernatural power and proves that he has the ability to train the monsters he captures.

This Game Boy game spawned an animated television series which became an instant hit, first in Japan where it originated, and ultimately around the world, particularly in the United States. It was an installment of one of these series that on December 16, 1997, caused the incident of mass seizures in Japan where seven hundred children were hospitalized. They became seriously ill while viewing the Pokemon program, some say as a result of a mysterious *flashing* effect during the episode.

The immense success of both the game and the television program stimulated the back-to-back release of two Pokemon movies in April and May of 1998 and additional movies that continue to be released. All of the Pokemon productions share the same goal to train children how to become the number one Pokemon Master in the world.

Pokemon Trainer of Masters

This term "master" is a non-subtle, in-your-face, giveaway to the fundamental nature of Pokemon. Becoming a "master" is part of the vocabulary and goal orientation of Zen Buddhism, the New Age meditative arts, and other Eastern religions. It is also one of the motivating factors for many who are deeply involved in the occult.

According to occultic literature, the "master" is a teacher who has mastered the occult system of belief and is therefore qualified to teach others what he or she has learned. Make no mistake about it, the use of this word and a menagerie of other words and phrases used by the Pokemon creators, as we shall soon see, is no accident.

Pokemon is now the world's most popular instructor to children on how to enter into the dark domain of occultic power and practice. Pokemon's objective is to teach children how to use *powers* to capture and conquer various monsters. Then with their captured monsters in their pockets they increase their own *powers*. Fundamentally this is training our children how to enter into and participate in a world of demonic activities.

The goal, according to Pokemon, is to *gain powers* and to employ and to trust these powers to accomplish desired results. But what kind of powers are the children involved with this product being taught to seek? And how can parents feel comfortable with instruction being given to their children on capturing monsters to carry in their pockets? Further, we must ask, is it good to train children to trust powerful little creatures to manifest their *powers* to help the child in time of trouble or to accomplish their goals?

Pokemon Indoctrinator

A casual investigation into the rules, terms, and phraseology in the Pokemon instructions is a clear give away to the occultic nature and roots of the game.

One of the first steps a child playing Pokemon must take is to go on a search for a *psychic* Pokemon by the name of *Kadabra*. "Abracadabra," of course, is a word most of us grew up hearing sleight-of-hand magicians use in their acts. However, the term originated in the world of the black arts and was part of the vernacular used in the casting of spells and incantations.

The Pokemon *Kadabra* is owned by a very powerful telepathic Pokemon trainer named *Sabrina*. Sabrina has great *powers* at her disposal and children are instructed that they must also trust supernatural *powers* in order to capture *Kadabra*. The children preparing for this quest are instructed that they will have help in their effort from a *secret friend*, another Pokemon who is a ghost named *Haunter*.

The game continues, and with each new phase children are drawn deeper into the practical application of occultic skills and the indoctrination of psychological strategies that walk them into a world of spiritualistic experiences.

Pokemon the Messenger

The Pokemon television series' and movies' theme song is a rap with the lyrics

> I'll travel across the land
> Searching far and wide
> Each Pokemon to understand
> The power that's inside . . .
> Gotta catch 'em all!"

These lyrics sum up the goal that the game's producers hope children will make a central part of their lives. The intent is to provoke children to accumulate as many Pokemon creatures as possible, hopefully all one hundred and fifty-plus, and to learn how to draw upon the supernatural powers that reside in each of these *pocket monsters*.

Additionally, Pokemon's instructive themes tell children, "Carry your Pokemon with you and you are ready for anything! You've got the power in your hands, so use it!"

Unfortunately, millions of children are following this advice. One website critique of the Pokemon craze wrote of the children who carry their favorite monsters, like magical charms or fetishes in their pockets, trusting them to bring them power in times of need. The critique states:

> . . . Many do. It makes sense to those who watch the television show. In a recent episode, Ash, the ten-year-old boy hero had just captured his fifth little Pokemon. But that wasn't good enough, said his mentor. He must catch lots more if he wants to be a Pokemon Master. And the more he catches and trains the more power he will have for future battles. . . .
>
> So, Ash sets out again in search of more of the reclusive, power-filled, little Pokemon. His first step is to find the "psychic Pokemon" called Kadabra and snatch it from its telepathic, pink-eyed trainer, Sabrina.
>
> But Ash misunderstands the power of his opponent. When he and Sabrina meet for the fight, both hurl their chosen Pokemon into the air but only Kadabra evolves into a super-monster with a magic flash. The Pokemon ghost, Haunter, hides. "Looks like your ghost Pokemon got spooked," taunts Sabrina.
>
> Obviously, Ash did not understand the supernatural powers he had confronted. Neither do most young Pokemon fans today. Unless they know God and His warnings they cannot understand the forces that have captivated children around the world. And if parents underestimate the psychological

strategies behind its seductive mass marketing ploys they are likely to dismiss the Pokemon craze as harmless fun and innocent fantasy. In reality, the problem is far more complex.

Pokemon the Strategist

The lyrics, "Gotta catch 'em all," from the rap song on the Pokemon program, is also thematic of the marketing scheme of the Pokemon creators. Again, the game, television program, and the movies are simply brilliant marketing tools for the multi-million dollar line of Pokemon products.

And many parents are falling for it, as they say, "hook, line, and sinker." In fact, last year one Pokemon marketing strategy included the effort to search for "the ultimate Poke-Mom."

The following is a reprint of the Internet article on the Pokemon News Website on June 12, 2000:

Who Is The Ultimate PokeMom?

This has been the burning question on the tip of everyone's tongue since the "Ultimate PokeMom Search" began last year.

Thousands of entries later, we're pleased to announce the name of America's Ultimate PokeMom, Jane Smith of Hampton, New York (real name and hometown changed).

Three years ago, Jane Smith and her family were introduced to Pokemon by a Japanese cousin before the phenomenon hit America. Her son who was six-years-old at the time fell in love with Pokemon instantly. As Pokemon started to become a big part of her family's day to day life, Jane says that she discovered some unexpected benefits.

"Pokemon has helped my family tremendously," Jane said. "I began to notice that as my son became more involved in the tournaments and card trading, his skills . . . began to skyrocket. He would discover new words on the trading cards and look them up in the dictionary. He's even writing a book on Pokemon."

Jane [started] spending more time with her son, now nine, and daughter Brittany, in their Pokemon related activities. Jane would help her children by searching out new and more cards, making Pokemon Halloween costumes, and carpooling to the Pokemon league two days per week.

This month Jane was selected as America's "Ultimate PokeMom" out of 16,000 entries in a nationwide contest here at Pokemon World. Along with the trip to New York, Jane will get a day of pampering and a $1,000.00 holiday shopping spree at FAO Schwarz. Her family will cruise around Manhattan in an official Pokemobile, a yellow VW Beetle customized to resemble Pikachu [one of the Pokemon characters].

After answering five Pokemon trivia questions correctly in November, Jane was one of ten semi-finalists randomly selected to write a one hundred-word essay demonstrating her Poke-knowledge, Poke-dedication, and how Pokemon is part of her family.

Here are some excerpts from Jane's winning essay.

"Everyday my son crawls out of his Pokemon sheets and comforter with Pokemon on the walls, watches Pokemon cartoons, puts on a Pokemon shirt, Ash hat, and plays one of his many Pokemon Game Boy/Nintendo 64 games, and/or reads from a Pokemon book. Then it's off to school, where he and his friends pre-arrange Pokemon card trades.

"I take time to make Pokemon Halloween costumes, wrap Pokemon X-mas gifts, design Pokemon desktop themes, plan Pokemon birthday parties, stand in line at Toy's 'R' Us with my son so he could win MEW (a Pokemon character) for Game Boy, carpool to Pokemon League two times a week, and create new and original Pokemon cards with my kids —

all the while humming the Pokemon theme song.

"I have learned how to play the Pokemon Trading Card Game, which is fun because it entails both luck and skill. I recognize all 150 plus Pokemon and know about their evolutions and characteristics. I can decide which Pokemon to send out and understand the 'Hit Points.' I continue to learn more about the characters by playing twenty questions 'Guess that Pokemon' with my kids. I expand my knowledge by watching the cartoons with my kids."

Reading that article provides us with an elongated definition of the term *obsession*. And yet, the fact is, clearly many hundreds of thousands of parents are encouraging their children to immerse themselves in the world of Pokemon. The cost can be staggering, not only in the purchasing of the vast number of Pokemon products, but ultimately, in the damage it does to their children.

The genius behind the marketing of Pokemon is astonishing. Children are so captured by the commercial appeal of Pokemon that millions of them literally beg their parents for more and more of the games and gadgets. And moms and dads are listening, generating one of the most successful advertising and marketing schemes ever launched.

But, beyond the economics, what are the values, and more specifically, what are the belief systems that Pokemon is teaching these children?

The fact is, there is an undeniable emphasis on teaching children to fight, kill, poison, and to use psychic and occultic powers to accomplish their goals. Additionally, the world of Pokemon is teaching children that evolution, supernatural powers, and violence are all perfectly acceptable concepts.

Pokemon the Teacher

Most parents do not want their children learning the kinds of lessons fundamentally taught by the world of Pokemon, but few are aware of the spiritualistic nature of the principals taught and espoused by Pokemon.

One website exposing the dangers of Pokemon recently alluded to the beliefs and values promoted by the Pokemon games and programs. Under the title "How Pokemon and Magic Cards Affect the Minds and Values of Children," Berit Kjos wrote of one woman who captured the attention of the Pokemon promoters. He writes:

Susan Barns (real names not used) started seeking answers after her son asked a typical question, "Mom, can I get Pokemon cards? A lot of my friends from church have them." Much as she wanted Johnny to have fun with his friends, she gave a loving refusal. Johnny's tutor had already warned her that the Pokemon craze could stir interest in other kinds of occult, role-playing games such as Dungeons and Dragons. At the time, she wondered if the tutor had just overreacted to some harmless entertainment. After all, the cute, little Pokemon creatures looked nothing like the dark demonic creatures of D & D. But when she learned that a local Christian school had banned them because of their link to the occult, she changed her mind.

Later, during a recent party for Johnny, Susan heard two of the boys discussing their little pocket monsters. One said, "I'll just use my psychic powers." Already the world of fantasy had colored his real world. So, when some of the kids wanted to watch the afternoon Pokemon cartoon on television, Susan again had to say "no." It's not easy to be parents these days.

Helen Bates would agree. Back in 1995, her son's elementary school had found a new, exciting way to teach math. The school was using a program called, "Magic: the Gathering, The Role-Playing Game," which, like D & D, has built a cult following among people of all ages across the country.

Helen refused to let her son participate in the "Magic Club." But a classmate gave him one of the magic cards, which he shared with his mother. It was called "soul exchange" and pictured spirits rising from graves. Like all other cards in this ghastly game, it offered a morbid instruction, "Sacrifice a white creature."

"What does 'summon' mean?" he asked his mother after school one day.

"Summon? Why do you ask?"

He told her that during recess on the playground the children would "summon" the forces in the cards they collect by raising sticks into the air and saying, "Spirits enter me." They call it "being possessed."

Strange as it may sound to American ears, demonic possession is no longer confined to distant lands. Today, government schools from coast to coast are teaching students the skills once reserved for tribal witchdoctors or shamans in distant lands. Children everywhere are learning the pagan formulas for invoking "angelic" or demonic spirits through multi-cultural education, popular books, movies, and television. It is not surprising that deadly explosions of untamed violence suddenly erupt from "normal" teens across our land.

Occult role-playing games teach the same dangerous lessons. They also add a sense of personal power and authority through personal identification with godlike superheroes. Though the demonic realm hasn't changed, today's technology, media, and multi-cultural climate make it easier to access and harder than ever to resist its appeal.

Role-Playing and Psychological Addiction

The televised Pokemon show brings suggestions and images that set the stage for the next steps of entanglement. It beckons the young spectator to enter the manipulative realm of role-play where fantasy simulates reality and the buyer becomes a slave to their programmer.

Remember, in the realm of popular role-playing-games, whether it's Pokemon or other games, the child becomes the Master. As in contemporary witchcraft, he or she wields the power. Their arms, minds, or power symbol (the Pokemon or other action figure) becomes the channel for the spiritual forces. Children from Christian homes may have learned to say, "Thy will be done," but in the role-playing world this prayer is twisted into, "My will be done." God, parents, and pastors no longer fit into the picture fantasized by many children.

Psychologists have warned that role-playing can cause the participants to actually experience, emotionally, the role being played. Again, "the child becomes the Master." Or, so it seems to the player.

Actually, the programmer who writes the rules is the master. And when the game includes occultism and violence, the child hero is trained to use his or her spiritual power to kill, poison, evolve, and destroy . . . over and over. Not only does this repetitive practice blur the line between reality and fantasy, it also sears the conscience and causes the player to devalue life. The child learns to accept unthinkable behavior as normal.

To be a winner in this system, the committed player must know and follow the rules of the game. Obedience becomes a reflex, strengthened by instant rewards or positive reinforcement. The rules and rewards force the child to develop new habits and patterned responses to certain stimuli. Day after day, this powerful psychological process manipulates the child's thoughts, feelings, and actions until his or her personality changes and, as many parents confirm, interest in ordinary family life begins to wither away.

You may have recognized the preceding terms as those often used by behavioral psychologists. They point to a sophisticated system of operant conditioning or behavior modification. The child must operate his own intelligent mind to learn the complete rules. But after learning the rules, the programmed stimuli produces conditioned responses to the player. These responses become increasingly automatic, a reflex action. Naturally, this can lead to psychological addiction, a craving for greater (and more expensive) thrill and darker forces. . . .

Let me acknowledge here that the facts present parents with some considerable challenges to think through. All parents know that it is difficult to teach restraint to children regarding popular trends.

Therefore, instead of just saying, "No!" when our children want to participate in areas of entertainment that we know are harmful, we should teach them *why* they should choose against it.

But, in order to teach children, parents must first be willing to teach themselves.

Chapter 3

Pokemon
and Growing Concerns

"Church Raises Red Flag Over Pokemon"
Toledo Black, December 18, 1999

When it comes to the Pokemon trading card craze, Rev. Clapsadde would probably love to "catch 'em all." But he's no fan of the fad. In fact, the children's pastor of Solid Rock Ministries won't allow the popular cards in the church, unless they're about to be laid on the altar by repentant church kids.

"Pokemon cards," he said, "teach children that they are masters of their universe, a principal that conflicts with the sovereignty of God and the commandments to honor their parents."

"Monsters Among Us"
Fox/AP, November 3, 1999

The Reverend Joe Chambers of Charlotte, North Carolina, says the whole scheme of [Pokemon] is based on "sorcery and witchcraft . . . it teaches about how the characters gain power from crystals."

He says it's the same type of thing that the two teens at Columbine High School dabbled in prior to their shooting rampage.

"Pokepervs?"
ABC/Reuters, February 22, 2000

The principal Roman Catholic archdiocese in New Mexico attacked the hugely popular Pokemon cartoon series saying the characters incited violence and sexual perversity among children.

"Christian School Bans Kid's Craze"

New Zealand Herald, February 23, 2000

A Christian school has banned Pokemon, claiming the toys are laced with references to the occult and promotes anti-social behavior.

The principal stated promotional material describes various Pokemon characters as "stubborn, headstrong, quibbling, self-centered, vindictive, obnoxious, hormonal, sexually preoccupied, evil, thieving, and cross-dressing."

Principal Burgess was also concerned that the game emphasized supernatural powers and poisoning your opponent. "It needs to be spelled out for parents that this is not just disruption. It is far more insidious."

"Pastor Calls Pokemon 'Poison'"

Denver Post, August 14, 1999

A minister used a blowtorch and a sword during a church service this week to drive home his belief that Pokemon games and toys are only sugar-coated instruments of the occult and evil.

"No, to Pokemon Cards"

AP, Los Angeles, California, January 2000

Dozens of junior high schools throughout Southern California are expelling Pokemon from their campuses.

School administrators claim that Pokemon card trading has been the source of numerous incidents of violence among students during school hours. Children trading their favorite cards have not been able to hold their fervor or enthusiasm in check. According to school officials, the trading sessions have been the cause of a number of serious outbreaks of violence. Most commonly reported among the incidents are fights, yelling, and even several stabbing incidents.

Above are only a few of the growing numbers of reports surfacing all over America and around the world where children are involving themselves with the world of Pokemon.

But why are these ministers and rapidly increasing numbers of public and private school administrators reacting so outspokenly to the Pokemon phenomena?

Alas, the truth is that even those who have no background in or knowledge of the occult and aberrant behavioral problems do recognize that the actions and attitudes manifesting in the atmosphere created by interaction with Pokemon pose a potential threat.

Anyone who is willing to look just below the surface and willing to do a bit of homework can readily discover the New Age message and occultic nature of this phenomenon.

Pokemon the Characters

As we have observed, there are now over one hundred and fifty-one Pokemon that children are taught to conquer and capture. A brief look at some of the characters exposes the type of powers that children are being encouraged to learn about, to experience, and to use.

The following Pokemon and the accompanying descriptions are taken straight from a Pokemon Website:

Hypno
Hypno survives by putting its prey to sleep and consuming their dreams. It can get sick from absorbing bad dreams.
Type: Psychic

Ivysaur
Once Bulbasaur reaches level 16, they evolve into the more pow-

erful Ivysaur. These are a Grass/Poison combination, giving them twice the strength of single type Pokemon. Given enough experience, Ivysaur will evolve into Venusaur.
Type: Grass/Poison

Alakazam

Experts believe that his brain is as powerful as any super computer. Its incredible psychic abilities back up that belief.
Type: Psychic

Gastly

No Pokemon have an advantage over these ghost-like Pokemon, making them valuable assets to any collector. Over time, Gastly evolves into Haunter and Gengar.
Type: Ghost

Abra

Abra lacks attack abilities but their power to teleport their way out of trouble makes them difficult to capture. They evolve into Kadabra.
Type: Psychic

Jynx

Jynx has an unusual combination of Ice and Psychic characteristics. Its evolution is not known at this time, though its powers do grow stronger over time.
Type: Ice/Psychic

Magnemite

Magnemite uses their electrical powers to paralyze and confuse their opponents before shocking them into submission.
Type: Electric

Jigglypuff

This Pokemon is rare and deceptive. Although they're cute and

cuddly in appearance, their attack will send even the toughest Pokemon into dreamland.
Type: Normal

Omastar
Scientist as yet, have little data about this resurrected Pokemon.
Type: Rock/Water

Mewtwo
The Pokemon lab tried to create the perfect fighting machine and they succeeded, perhaps too well. Mewtwo is extremely hostile.
Type: Psychic

Nidoran
One of the few two-gender Pokemon who attacks with poisonous barbs that protrude from their backs.
Type: Poison

These are but a few of the characters that children are having *fun* with and learning how to use their powers to manipulate.

Please notice some key character facets attributed to these Pokemon playmates: *psychic, poison, powers, evolution, haunt, ghost, teleport, paralyze, confuse, eliminate, hostile, and shock into submission.*

No right thinking adult is going to consider the character traits and the activities associated with these creatures as *healthy.* Most parents do not want their children participating in activities with playmates who are psychic, poisonous, haunters, hostile, and who practice killing, shocking others into submission, or eliminating their opponents with the use of psychic powers.

Additionally, as previously mentioned, the premise of the

entire Pokemon agenda is to bring children into a role-playing fantasy game. It has been repeatedly proven that many children, as well as teens and young people, once initiated into the world of role-playing games soon begin to lose the capacity to distinguish between the real world and fantasy. Many parents have already contacted me expressing their concern that just such a problem has developed in their children as a result of Pokemon.

Anton Levey, founder and leader of the Church of Satan in Southern California, has stated that the best way to indoctrinate young lives with the occult is through fantasy role-playing games.

Of course, someone always poses the question, "Oh, but didn't you fantasize during games as a young boy while playing Cowboys and Indians, or Cops and Robbers?"

I like the answer to such a question provided by David Benoit in his book *Who's Watching the Playpen?* He writes:

. . . Yes, I pretended to shoot bad guys, but that was different. Let me explain:

1. When we were growing up, the Cops and Robbers were adults. As kids, we could not totally identify with the characters. Today, television bombards children with images of children doing the killing, not just adults. So children now see that as "normal." They can totally relate to the character. We are seeing a rise in violent crimes performed by younger [and younger] children. . . .

2. Television today is much more graphic in its depiction of killing. When we were growing up we saw an Indian shot off a horse. You heard the blast and saw the Indian fall. Today, not only do you hear the blast, you actually see the person's face deteriorate as you pull the trigger. The cameras in old films were second person. You saw someone else shoot people. Now the camera is first person. The camera

angle puts you behind the gun barrel. You become the killer. . . .

Any parent who has raised small children understands their proclivity to respond to suggestion. In the Pokemon games and programs, the effort to bring children into the fantasy role-playing activity as violent and occultic participants is undeniable.

Pokemon Premise

The art of teaching, it has been said, is repetition. As children indulge themselves in the Pokemon action, they are repeatedly thrust into a role where concepts and the philosophical fundamentals of the New Age and the occult are reinforced in their thinking.

An illustration of this is how the participant repeatedly deals with various Pokemon characters which go through the process of *evolution*. For instance, the Pokemon Bulbasaur, a poison-type character, evolves into Ivysaur and Venusaur. A great number of other Pokemon creatures also go through this *evolutionary* process. Players who become proficient masters must be able to memorize these characters and their *evolutions*. Hence, a major part of the participant's vocabulary and the concepts are based on *evolution* as a factual reality in their world.

Humanism, a growing religion that deifies man and humanizes God, putting man at the center of his universe, has evolution as its fundamental doctrine. Humanists, New Agers, as well as many others involved in the black arts subscribe to this unscientific and unscriptural belief and are extremely evangelistic in their campaign to convert this generation to their way of thinking.

The evolutionary concepts repeatedly woven into the Pokemon games are teaching children that evolution is the natural order of creation and life. This fundamental assault upon the premise of biblical creation denies the creative influence of God in the universe. If children can be taught at an early age to explain away God, as evolution attempts to do, they can easily be taught that they have no responsibility to God.

Pokemon's premise is no different than that of Darwin, which is "only the strong survive." However, this is not what the Word of God teaches. God's Word, contrary to Pokemon, teaches children to love their enemies, not to attack and kill them. Christianity also embraces the biblical truth that the "meek shall inherit the earth," not that the most devious in the use of their *powers* are the victors.

Pokemon Roots

In teaching my children over the years how to discover the message behind the things they watch and read, I have ingrained in their thinking the fact that there is a root philosophy behind all art, literature, music, and programming. The secret to discovering the underlying message behind the entertainment value of such things is to listen for key words and phrases. Pokemon creators have made it quite easy to discover the basic message and values they wish to promote. In fact, the connection between the characteristics of individual Pokemon creatures corresponds precisely with New Age and occultic terminology.

Stones

A perfect example of this is the Pokemon named Eevee. This character can be *morphed* or changed into three different kinds of Pokemon by their trainers. However, their trainer must rely upon special *stones* in order to bring about the transformation. A trainer can use a "water stone, a thunder stone, or a fire stone" to accomplish the transformation.

A number of other Pokemon can be transformed only by

the use of certain stones as well, but the use of *stones* in order to transfer supernatural powers is as old as witchcraft and the occult. Many kinds of stones have been thought by occultists to have mediumistic capabilities.

New Age proponents believe that some stones, such as crystal, can give off energy that has the ability to heal and even transmit thoughts. All of us have heard of the "crystal ball" used by occultists as a medium to transmit information.

Psy-War

The Pokemon Psyduck is another character that resorts to the use of the paranormal to accomplish his will. Psyduck defeats his opponents by *mesmerizing them with a piercing stare and releasing a barrage of pent-up mental energy.* The New Age concept that parallels this ability falls under the heading of an *altered state of consciousness*.

New Agers, and clearly Pokemon, believe that mental powers can be transferred to accomplish one's desired end by an intense focusing upon that desire. The fact is, demonic forces can be summoned to participate in lives by those involved in occultic practices. Tragically, New Agers and others involved in the paranormal do not ascribe the results of such activity to the power of demons, but are deceived into believing that their own power is at work.

Dream Robbing

One Pokemon, Hypno, has a unique ability to deal with his opponents that is no less occultic in nature. Hypno is able to make his opponents go to sleep so that he can drain their powers by stealing their dreams. This ability has its roots in the shamanistic world of the ancient American Indians. Many early tribal rituals focused on *dream robbing* in order to heal the sick, deliver the afflicted, cleanse the souls of the anguished, and relieve numerous maladies.

New Agers today are fond of a device made by contemporary shamans called a *dream catcher*. This device is supposed to help individuals dictate the kinds of dreams they have.

Energy

Zobat, another Pokemon, enters battle with the strategy to drain and steal his opponent's energy. A number of Pokemon share the ability to interfere with the energy centers of their enemy.

This preoccupation with using psychic powers to drain an opponent's energy is rooted in Eastern religion and New Age philosophy. The focus upon "energy" is, in itself, a New Age concept. They teach that energy can be altered by one's own will or by the concentrated will of others. The Hindus have a teaching that proposes each of us have seven energy centers within our bodies called *chakras*.

Zobat clearly uses his powers to focus on his enemy's chakras in order to achieve his purposes.

More, So Much More . . .

The reliance of Pokemon upon the paranormal, New Age philosophy, and occultic practices is undeniable and a Christian's involvement with it is indefensible. A casual look at the one hundred and fifty-plus Pokemon and the powers they use to accomplish their ends reveals numerous other New Age and occultic techniques that they teach its players to draw upon. Included among these are references to and/or reliance upon:

Elements — witches believe they can control the forces of nature such as earth, wind, stones, fire, and water.

Visualization — the belief that material reality can be achieved by the power of the mind.

Transpersonal Education — a learning process that teaches how to achieve an extreme level of knowledge by tapping into a higher power beyond the five senses.

Taoism — this is a religion teaching its adherents that *forces* can be exercised upon the world of the supernatural to alter its reality.

Wicca — the official religion of witches. Among their doctrine is the belief that the elements of nature can and should be used in incantations to reach their desired results.

Medium Reliance — the dependence upon a person or object to be a conductor for supernatural spirits or powers.

Reincarnation — (psychic evolution) a belief in a cycle of life determined by conduct and actions.

Hypnosis — an altered state of consciousness attained through the focused yielding of one's will to another.

Parapsychology — an effort to combine facets from the world of science with that of the spirit world. This combination is supposed to create a supernatural channel for trafficking in psychic maneuvers, telepathic activity, healing, or harming others with psychic power.

Guided Imagery — defines the activities of surrendering one's mind or imagination to a "teacher" (or spirit) in order to achieve a particular goal or to receive a greater revelation of paranormal, supernatural, or New Age concepts.

Spiritism — a belief that the world of spirits and/or "entities" are the sole manipulators of the unseen world and that humans can interact with these powers to determine outcomes in material reality.

Earth Temples — people involved in New Age and like religions are convinced that certain locations are the center for psychic energies or powers. The pyramids of Egypt and rock formations of Stonehenge, in Great Britain, are prime examples of this. Entities living near Earth Temples draw upon this power to fulfill objectives.

Alchemy — the use of "deity-like" attributes to transform the basic nature of an object.

Each of the categories mentioned, at some level, have a link and counterpart associated with the Pokemon game and products. Some of the parallels in Pokemon are subtle, while others are extremely obvious.

Pokemon Protection

Players of the game are constantly encouraged to capture as many Pokemon as possible. Not only do these creatures guarantee the participant more power, but they also act as *protectors* of the player.

In the world of wizardry, sorcery, and Satanism, there are similar objects that adherents are encouraged to carry with them, just as children are encouraged to carry their Pokemon (*pocket monsters*) with them. Those items include:

Charms — an object worn to avert danger from spells or magic.

Talisman — an object that has supernatural protective qualities.

Amulet — an object or item to ward off evil and to bring safe passage and protection.

One website that focuses on helping children learn how to improve their Pokemon skills states, *"So, Children, carry your Pokemon with you and you're ready for anything. . . . You've got the power in your hands. . . . So use it!"*

Children are being taught to trust Pokemon when they are in trouble or have problems. The constant emphasis for players to capture the maximum number of Pokemon creates a driving frenzy for children to "do whatever is necessary" to get more Pokemon, in order to gain more *power*.

Pokemon Psychology

The growing obsession of children involved in Pokemon to collect as many Pokemon related products as possible is fueled by the psychology of the game.

The fact is, the Pokemon creators have discovered the profitable marketing genius of coupling a popular video game and a television series/movies with a product line. Billions of dollars are being spent by compliant parents attempting to appease the growing appetite of their children who beg for each new Pokemon product.

And the line of Pokemon products is constantly increasing. One website advertises the latest Pokemon products currently available. Among these varied items are:

- Kraft's Pokemon Action Flipz cheese slices
- Nintendo's Pokemon Stadia Bundle — the official 3-D Fighting Kit of Pokemon Masters
- Golden Books popular line of Pokemon books
- Pokemon Collector Marbles
- Kraft Pokemon macaroni and cheese
- Pokemon World Enhanced CD with the Pokemon theme song
- Hew Topps Pokemon trading cards
- Pokemon Lollipops
- Pokemon Project Studio
- Pokemon Battle Figures
- Official Pokemon Players Guide
- Official Pokemon Book Collection
- Guide on Pokemon: 2 B.A. Master
- Pokemon Rummy Card Game
- Pokemon activity books with Pokemon Tales For Kids
- The Pokemon Game Link Cable

This is just a partial list of available Pokemon products and does not list the Pokemon clothes, décor, educational products, and dozens of other items marketed under the Pokemon logo.

Pokemon the Promoter

It is imperative that parents who care about the spiritual,

emotional, and psychological well-being of their children look very closely at the spiritual and philosophical message that lies behind Pokemon. Do not be deceived into believing that children are unaffected by the constant bombardment of occultic, humanistic, and New Age concepts and practices that they are exposed to and encouraged to participate in through involvement with the world of Pokemon.

The message being taught by this insidious series of games, movies, and television programs is diametrically opposed to the message that faithful Christian parents are attempting to instill in their children. As we shall see in a coming chapter of this book, God's Word goes far beyond simple warnings against our involvement in such activities. God demands that His people refrain from any and all participation in, practice and even tolerance of the dark world of occultic activities, errant philosophies, false religions, sorcery, and witchcraft, But as we can now see, all of these are being promoted through the growing influence of Pokemon.

Chapter 4

The Agenda

There can be no doubt but that television has become one of the primary sources of information on how children can become involved in New Age and occultic beliefs and lifestyles. It has also been a major tool of choice for carrying out a satanic agenda craftily designed to ensnare America's children in a web of witchcraft and sorcery.

While many of the producers and creators of children's programs may not be personally involved in any of these dark philosophies, they have without a doubt, discovered how to appeal to the natural curiosity about the supernatural that is so strong in children.

Yet, in order for parents to understand the constant spiritual assault that their children are under, they must first understand the great spiritual battle that is being waged for the heart and soul of their children. The battlefield of this ongoing conflict is in the mind.

It is little wonder that the forces of evil have chosen the medium of television from which to launch their primary assault upon children and young people. Most parents in our culture have decided to use television as the primary source of entertainment for their children. It quiets children and can settle the constant arguing of siblings while a parent can go on with their business without worrying about where their children are. Television has become the babysitter of choice for most parents.

The truth is, however, no one, child or adult, can remain

unaffected by the nonstop bombardment of the messages they are exposed to during thousands of hours of television viewing. It is an alarming but true statistic that the average American child will watch between eighteen and twenty thousand hours of television by the time he or she graduates from high school. During that time, they will witness over thirteen thousand killings while watching the television, not to mention the sexual perversity, crime, profanity, and other valueless activities which are central themes of much programming.

Concerned parents need to be aware that many, if not most, of the programs created for their children are full of references to and characters involved in witchcraft and the occult. In days past, Saturday morning cartoons were far more innocent. Mickey Mouse, Daffy Duck, Bugs Bunny, and Popeye have been replaced with infinitely more sinister characters. Unfortunately, the nature of these characters is masked behind the fact that they are often cute, cuddly, warm, little creatures that children and parents have trouble resisting.

However, woven through these cartoons is a story line laced with telepathy, psychic phenomena, Eastern religions, crystal powers, witchcraft, ESP, sorcery, and casting of spells.

Pokemon is only a late comer to the Saturday morning demonic lineup. The past few years have witnessed the occult propaganda machine, with the same anti-Christian themes, march shows like "Teenage Mutant Ninja Turtles," "He-Man"/ "She-Ra," "Care Bears," "Gummi Bears," "The Smurfs," "My Little Pony," and a host of others across our television screens.

Of course, the more popular cartoons have produced in their wake a multitude of other products, toys, movies, video games, stuffed animals, breakfast foods, snacks, and clothing. Each of these further reinforces the ungodly concepts of the program into children.

It cannot be stressed enough that children do have a very naive fascination with things supernatural. For most of these children, television is their first introduction into the dark, deceptive, and destructive world of the occult

Trapped!

The television and movie industry cannot escape their complicity in the spiritual entrapment of our children. As young minds are influenced at an early age by programming like Pokemon and its new counterpart for even younger children, Digimon, they develop an appetite for more of the dark philosophies that have entertained them since their youth. With an ever-expanding market available to them, producers, writers, and creators of movies and television have vigorously pumped out the kind of sordid programming demanded by the insatiable appetite for the occultic material. And the nonstop barrage of spiritualistic entertainment is having a devastating effect on this generation.

In a special report released to several national secular publications in the fall of 1999, a reporter named Catherine Rogers revealed a bit of the impact that this kind of programming is having. Her article was entitled "Wicca Casts Spell on Teenage Girls." She writes: ". . . In their universal quest for self-empowerment, a devilish number of teenage girls have become enchanted by the female-friendly but retrograde culture of witchcraft. . . ."

This reporter is absolutely correct in her observation that teens, both girls and boys, are searching for something to fill their lives. This search for meaning begins early and reaches its peak in the teen years. It is during these tender ages when children and young people are more susceptible to the voices that promise them fulfillment and purpose for their lives. When the occultic message of programming like Pokemon becomes a central focus in the life of a child it prepares him to later accept its message as a reality of his own.

Millions of today's teens have grown up consuming a steady

diet of witchcraft and the occult without receiving much biblical instruction about its deadly dangers.

The facts in Miss Rogers' article are extremely observant as they relate to why so many young people, especially teenage girls, are flocking into witchcraft and the occult.

Her article continues:

> ... Before sixteen year-old Jess lights candles on the small altar in the corner of her bedroom each night, she says her prayers. "Hail Fair Moon, ruler of the night, guard me and mine until the light. Hail Fair Sun, ruler of the day, make the morn light my way."
>
> On her altar are four porcelain chalices representing the elements of air, water, fire, and earth. Each contains more petals, semi-precious stones, melted candle wax, and dried leaves. They rest on the corners of a five-pointed star. And Jess has a frog she says symbolizes "spirit" and "life" that sits on point five of the pentagram. Here she performs rituals and casts spells.
>
> Jess is one of the growing number of American teenage girls who practice Wicca or witchcraft. In the last five years Hollywood has produced films including *Practical Magic* and *The Craft,* celebrating such cults and featuring hip actresses Nicole Kidman, Sandra Bullock, and "Party of Five's" Neve Campbell as witches. Primetime TV has cashed in with its own witchy programming. "Sabrina the Teenage Witch," "Buffy the Vampire Slayer," and "Charmed" all feature young females with magical powers. The character of Felicity, on the program of the same name broadcast on the Warner Brother's Network, has a Wiccan roommate. And teen witches have cast nasty spells on the popular series, "X-Files." ...

It is easy to see the trend of many of today's hottest television programs and movies as a simple continuation of the programming today's teen received while growing up in the 1980s and '90s. Only now, those things that were once "just kid's entertainment" have become the virtual lifestyle of millions of these young people. No longer is it just children's television programming. This has become the stuff they live for.

Continuing the article that Miss Rogers writes:

> . . . *Teen Witch: Wicca for a New Generation,* a recent book by Silver Ravenwolf has sold more copies for occult publisher Llewellyn than any other in its ninety-five year history, according to publicist, Jamie Schumacher. And it's not just media hype either. Danny Aguirre runs a Christian hot-line at Berkeley, California-based Spiritual Counterfeits Project. He says, "In the last six months, I have received more inquiries about Wicca than any other religion in the ten years I have worked here." The demographics of the callers? "All teenage girls," says Aguirre.

I should also point out that it is now reported that "Satanism" is currently the fastest growing religion in the United States. The phenomenal inrush of young people into the religion accounts for its unprecedented growth.

It should also be noted that those involved in witchcraft become extremely upset when one confuses their religion with that of the "Satanists." Witches reject the idea of a personal devil. However, from a biblical perspective, both religions stem from the same source and share the same god, the Father of Lies (John 8:44).

Looking again at the revealing article, we read:

> . . . As teens begin to ask questions about life and religion, they are turning in surprising numbers to witchcraft for answers. Drawn by Wicca's focus on a feminine deity, nature worship, and self-empowerment, many young women

have rejected traditional faiths as male-dominated, environmentally unfriendly, and morally limiting. Critics of Wicca, however, fear that if teen Wiccans ignore the dangers of the occult in their quests for meaning and satisfaction, they may well be putting themselves in harm's way. . . .

Once again, I must point out the fact that we live in a world where, as never before, children and teens are searching for something worthwhile. And, yet, the values that many parents are allowing television programs and entertainment to drive into their children's psyche are simply preparing them to be converts to the host of occultic messages being preached by the New Age prophets, whose primary pulpit is children's programming, such as Pokemon.

Another glance at the article on Wicca and its attraction for teenage girls reiterates this point.

. . . Fritz Jung and Wren Walker, practicing Wiccans who live in Clearwater, Florida, maintain that their website is the busiest religious site in the world. In a web survey conducted on that site in September, sixty percent of respondents were under thirty and sixty-two percent were females. [The same] survey found that ninety percent of Wiccan respondents were white and well educated. . . .

Clearly, as this reporter discovered, there is a rapidly expanding fascination with the occult. This growing appetite is not the result of "Johnny-come-lately" cultural trends. The intense efforts of spiritual forces to saturate children's entertainment with the message that promotes participation in the occult as exciting, fun, and fulfilling has produced results.

Parents who allow and facilitate their children's preoccupation with Pokemon-type activities are sowing seeds that will eventually take root and bear fruit. Children are being conditioned by their interplay with the demonic entities of Pokemon to believe that they can trust psychic phenomena, place their confidence in the strengths of spirits, and have fulfilling relationships with mystical powers. As these children grow older, it is little wonder that the first place that they begin to look for something to fill the spiritual void in their lives is the occult.

These truths are borne out in the article by Miss Rogers when she writes:

> ... "There is a great spiritual hunger among kids out there," says Bob Walisgewski, manager of the youth culture department at the conservative group, Focus on the Family. "I understand the initial draw of Wicca for girls. For a young teenage girl with no spiritual roots, if Wicca promises them power, I can see how they would be tempted. . . ."

Mr. Walisgewski's observations are correct. As previously stated, there is a great and demanding spiritual hunger among teens. He is also correct in his statement regarding the powerful temptations that Wicca can be to teenage girls. But the most important fact of his statement is his stressing the point that Wicca is an attraction to teenage girls "with no spiritual roots."

Parents who believe that their children will be protected from any temptation to enter the world of the occult because their children were raised in a Christian home need to take note. What many people mean when they say they have a Christian home is that they were raised believing the Bible and the tenets of the Christian faith. Others mean that they, as parents, take their children to church on Sundays.

While I plan to deal with how to protect children from satanic and occultic influences in their lives in another chapter of this book, do allow me one observation here. Taking our children to church for a couple of hours a week and exposing them to the Christian faith while simultaneously allowing our children to participate in occultic activities and be entertained by demonic programs and games does not develop godly, biblical, spiritual roots. Such a dichotomy in our religious beliefs tends only to confuse children and to create within them deep doubts about the legitimacy of their parent's Christian convictions.

Christianity is far more than a religious philosophy. In fact, Americanized Christianity, mental consent without submission to the Lordship of Christ in every area of life, is so foreign to biblical Christianity that it could easily be classified as a cult.

It should not come as a surprise to many so-called Christian parents who failed to teach their children God's Word while allowing them to be brainwashed by demonic entertainment, when their children turn to witchcraft and the occult as they become teenagers and young adults.

Such a statement may infuriate many nominal Christian parents. However, the journalist who authored the article on "Wicca and Teen Girls" made some further observations explaining just why young people feel attracted to this evil religion. She writes:

> . . . After all, despite a history of cauldrons and Satan worship, modern witches claim that Wicca is a positive and life-affirming religion. The Wiccan Rede, an ethic that is often cited, directs, "Do what you will but harm none." Wiccans also claim to believe in the Law of Threefold, which states whatever you do comes back to you three times as strong.
>
> "Adherents usually follow their own path," says Ravenwolfe, "which allows for great subjectivity." As [Wiccan leaders] note, "in a circle there are no absolutes — no rights and wrongs."

Please notice the consistency of the philosophy promoted by

the Pokemon creatures who do whatever is necessary in order to win, regardless of right or wrong, and that of the Wiccans. The Wiccan's creed, "Do what you will, but harm none," gives a license to participants to disregard moral restraints and to "do what comes naturally." Anyone who protests against participation in immoral or unethical behavior is simply told, "I'm not harming anyone, so mind your own business!"

The religious humanist whose creed also rejects absolutes is extremely compatible with the same philosophy shared by occultists, Satanists, New Agers, and witches. Something is wrong in their world only if it is wrong for them as individuals.

The religious beliefs of all of these groups are in direct conflict with the teachings of Christianity. As we shall see, God's Word is not subjective. Right and wrong do not change with the circumstances or with cultural trends, and according to the Scriptures, it is never right to do wrong.

In the world of Pokemon and that of the New Agers, the occultist's and the Wiccan's right and wrong are determined by individual choice. This deadly philosophy is being ingrained in the thinking of millions of children whose parents are failing to get involved in their child's Saturday morning television viewing habits.

The article, which we have only printed in bits and pieces, concludes with these words along the same line of thought:

> ... Since Wiccans deny a single standard of truth and laws of right and wrong, how do they know the difference between what is harmful and not harmful?
>
> Alex Sabders, a flamboyant publicist and self-named "King of the Witches," who died in 1988, wrote that "a thing is good for me until I feel it's not right for me." The witch, Stewart Farron, elaborates, "The witches own conscience must be the final arbiter."

Art Lindsey of the C. S. Lewis Institute, the Washington-based think-tank focusing on different religions, notes that for Wiccans "there is no objective evil that someone ought not do. There is no ought in Wicca — it is all based on subjective feeling."

"Making your own rules and doing what feels good naturally appeals to inexperienced teens," says one eleventh grader. "Wicca allows me to create my own religion and that suites me. It's malleable."

And all the help she needs to engage in this witchcraft is right at her fingertips on the Internet. . . .

The reporter notes that "making your own rules" and doing what feels good appeals to teens. But the fact is, for anyone at any age who has yet to personally discover the liberating truths of the Lord Jesus Christ, making your own rules and being your own god is an attractive proposition.

The all-revealing truth about humanity cut off from God is summarized in the words of the eleventh grader who has created her own spiritual reality in the world of witchcraft. She stated, "Wicca allows me to create my own religion." In other words, she will dictate the principles by which she lives. However, the sad fact is that this young woman and millions like her are living in a dark world whose grip upon their lives will slowly tighten until they have no life left at all.

As Paul the apostle wrote of others who were living in a world of spiritual deception, they promise themselves liberty while living in great bondage (2 Pet. 2:19).

Tools of the Trade

In recognizing the similarities between the nature of witchcraft and the occult with that of Pokemon, it is impossible to escape the conclusion that Satan will use any and all means necessary to entrap young hearts. As it is in the world of illicit drug use, so it is with those who gradually become addicted to occultic activity. Most hardcore drug addicts will readily confess that they started by using those drugs considered less powerful. Marijuana and alcohol are often the starting points for diving into the use of more potent and deadly drugs, such as heroin and cocaine.

No parent really believes their child could actually end up as a mass murderer or suicide victim as a result of their early tampering in the occult through games and programs like Pokemon. However, statistics prove, as do countless personal testimonies, that many whose lives have been destroyed by participating in the occult started by childish dabblings in seemingly innocent activities.

Some years ago, a nineteen-year-old young man named Sean Sellers was found guilty of murdering his parents while they slept. Sean was recently executed in Oklahoma for his crimes.

"As a young boy," Sean testifies, "I got interested in stories about the supernatural." One day a babysitter started sharing books with him about the occult. Sean says, "I, like a lot of other kids I knew, started feeling strangely attracted to the occult."

When he turned twelve, Sean was introduced to fantasy role-playing games. Sean's experience took place a few years ago before the fantasy role-playing game of Pokemon was introduced. Nevertheless, Sean Sellers ultimately came upon another game which some have alluded to as the "Pokemon of the '80s and early '90s." The game, still popular among children who are outgrowing Pokemon, is known as Dungeons & Dragons. The similarities between the techniques, goals, and objectives used in Pokemon and D & D are striking.

The Sean Sellers' story is one of the most graphic and heartbreaking any parent will ever hear. He tells of his slide into rebellion against society, his parents, God, and, ultimately, all that is holy. Sean says his early involvement of simply dabbling in occultic games eventually led to his total enslavement to evil. "I performed," he says, "rituals covered in blood, sometimes mixed with blood and urine, and began taking drugs. I thought I had at last found what I was looking for. I was wrong. Now as a result of all I did in Satanism, I am condemned to die."

When reading of the degradation and of the life of horror that Sean Sellars was ultimately driven to, one hopes that he was an exception. However, as more and more children and young people across America are going on killing rampages of their schoolmates, teachers, friends, and families, the experience of Sean is looking more like the rule rather than the exception.

Chapter 5

Pokemon Obsession

Unless a parent has a child who has become obsessively attracted to or involved in Pokemon it may be difficult for them to understand why an increasing number of Christian leaders and parents are becoming so concerned. The fact is, Pokemon is an affront and an assault upon the basic message of the Christian faith. It focuses on a behavioral and belief system that are in absolute conflict with the Word of God.

Pokemania, as many are now calling the children's obsession with Pokemon, instructs children through inference and example to steal, deceive, fight, and physically injure in order to achieve the objective to *"catch 'em all."*

The movies are no different than the television series in their fundamental theme. While there is an overriding plot that focuses upon world peace, the subtler message focuses on the use of psychic powers. Characters in the movie on the surface appear to attempt to bring resolution to conflicts, but the means and the ends of the philosophy being promoted are disturbing to those who know their Bible and understand manipulation.

Berit Kjos is a website critic of the Pokemon movies. He compares the message and teaching technique with that of the secular humanists and New Agers.

... This conflict between human nature and noble ideas is vital to the worldwide education programs and the Pokemon version of "edutainment" fits right in. Through entertainment it instills new beliefs and values . . . and it fills each child's mind with the same violent images, nice–sounding sentiments, and unspoken needs to resolve the inner conflict between two opposites. The child becomes part of a like-minded group which reinforces the new collective values. Meanwhile, the child has too much fun to think rationally about what's happening to him. . . .

In short, the creators of Pokemon and a vast number of other children's programs have learned that the most efficient way to indoctrinate young minds is by wrapping the message in story lines and game objectives that, on one hand, are fun-filled entertainment, and on the other hand, very effective propaganda-riddled productions. This brainwashing technique is reinforced when the focus of the brainwashing, in this case children, shares the Pokemon adventure with a group of their peers. In this setting, each individual shares in the "common experience" and more readily accepts the premise.

This dualistic approach of diversion and enforcement by the Pokemon marketers has proven overwhelmingly successful in not only the selling of Pokemon products, but in the assimilation of the Pokemon message by children.

Pokemon movie critic Mr. Kjos further states:

. . . While children hear and proclaim ideals such as kindness and cooperation they are led into a virtual Pokemon world of power, battles, cheating, and greed. But don't think that those mental images come from their own minds. The Pokemon movie and television episodes do not just stir the imagination, they steer it. Unlike the simple toys of past centuries that prompted the child to depend on their own imagination, the movies linked to toys and games create a context for the child's imagined experience. This context determines how they use their toys, games, and gadgets. In other words, today's entertainment industry feeds, manipulates, and directs the child's mind and imagination. . . .

I applaud Mr. Kjos' keen observations. Pokemon has taken indoctrination techniques to a whole new level. While it is true that many public educators have taught subjective values clarification and other humanistic propaganda in the classrooms for several decades, the designers of Pokemon have succeeded in camouflaging their video propaganda in, what to children, is an almost irresistible format.

There is a global effort engineered by a spiritual conspiracy of which the prophets of old long ago forewarned us. It's an effort to conform a generation's thinking, attitudes, values, and religious convictions to an ever-evolving universal standard. While many non-Christians and even some Christians are not aware of the prophetic significance of such statements, it behooves serious believers to understand how penetrating these efforts have become.

Pokemon's approach to conflict-resolution is in perfect harmony with the goals of New Agers and humanists. Of course, the desire to resolve differences and conflicts in itself is commendable. However, the popular approach to conflict-resolution preached in the Pokemon movies and television series is really after more than teaching children to resolve conflict. The ultimate goal is to conform young children to think and act as a "collective" rather than as individuals. The final aim of such indoctrination is to teach conformity through compromise.

It may sound socially healthy to compromise for the sake of resolution. But the fact is, when it comes to true biblical values and Christian convictions, Christians have far too much to lose to compromise. Unfortunately, the politically-correct position today is extremely anti-Christian. The trend in the public arena is to blame social conflicts, political meanness, and religious injustice on the intolerant beliefs of people who claim to be Christians and believe in biblical absolutes. The politically correct say, *"You Christians who subscribe to the belief in biblical absolutes and refuse to give up your convictions and modify your positions are offensive and divisive!"*

Just beneath the surface and between the lines of Pokemon rhetoric lies the message that the real pathway to unity among mankind and the road to world peace can be achieved if all ideologies and religions will simply move to "common ground." Of course, it is necessary, according to these social engineers, for each of us to be more understanding of one another's pain, more tolerant of other's views, and less dogmatic in our own beliefs. In short, this culture's overall solution to all of our social conflict is to simply compromise.

However, Christians are to submit themselves to a much higher authority than any "collective social order." The disciples of Christ are committed irrevocably to cling to the eternal, inerrant, infallible Word of God. We cannot surrender one iota of scriptural truth nor compromise biblical principles, not even to achieve a dreamed-of social Utopia.

For a Christian to accept the premise of the Pokemon message it would require he surrender innumerable biblical convictions such as the deity of Christ, the infallibility of the Word of God, and the belief that salvation can only be attained by grace through faith in the death and resurrection of God's Son, the Lord Jesus Christ. It would also mandate that the Christian give up their firm belief in the eventual return and reign of the Lord Jesus Christ on the Earth. These are fundamental tenets of the Christian's faith. If they are given up, then the entire Christian belief system would collapse.

If one believes that the Word of God is true, than it is virtually impossible for that individual to subscribe and submit to the philosophy and message woven into Pokemon.

Pocket Monster Magic

To illustrate this fact, let's define the Pokemon message.

Though many of the Pokemon family of characters appear to be fun-filled little creatures, the fact is they are, by admission of their creators, "pocket monsters." In fact, they are more than just monsters. These creatures exhibit the kind of power that classifies them as supernatural, spiritual entities. Another word for an entity in this context is *spirit*. In the world of biblical truth, there are only two kinds of spirits or angels.

There are *holy* angels and *unholy* angels. According to the Word of God, holy angels or spirits are available to God as messengers to do His bidding. These ministering spirits of righteousness appear throughout the Bible to fulfill their roles of obedience to God, bringing messages and comfort to His children (Heb. 1:14).

There are also the fallen angels, or demons, who are busy about their devious and deceptive agenda. These malevolent spirits go about attempting to hinder and debilitate the people of God. They also work in league with unredeemed humanity, spiritually blind people, in order to hinder their eyes being opened to the truths of God (Acts 26:18).

A casual investigation into the characters of Pokemon entities, with their supernatural, spiritualistic powers, reveals their diabolic nature. These "spirits" are not out fulfilling the divine mission of a holy God, nor are they out to minister to the people of God. Frankly, their entire focus, character, and agenda is in perfect harmony with what the Bible describes as the *forces of evil*.

Pokemon Power

The use of psychic powers to achieve desired ends is strictly forbidden in the Scriptures. This use of supernatural abilities is not a godly attribute, but a number of Pokemon like Mewtwo, Haunter, and Hypno are favorites among children because of their exciting demonstrations of psychic powers.

The word "psychic" has various connotations to different people, but the fundamental meaning is understood by most to be occultic in origin. The following definition is found in the Donning International Psychic Dictionary compiled by June G. Bletzer, Ph.D.

> . . . Psychic (ch`i or ki) energy — an intelligent, powerful, invisible force . . . capable of being controlled and directed by the human mind; 1. Capable of being **channeled** through the brain, palms, and eyes; 2. Can be transmitted through space into other living organisms and through matter; 3. Occurs when willed or occurs spontaneously; 4. Invisible energy living in all organisms and matter, connected throughout all the universes, psychic energy is an aspect of electricity . . . 6. Controlled and employed under certain conditions that mankind does not fully understand . . . tunes into the etheric world vibrational frequencies reaching from cosmic consciousness . . . 9. Transmits knowledge to mind, and manipulates matter . . . 10. Frequently comes from an intelligent powerful energy field known as highly evolved soul minds in invisible bodies. 12. A primordial form of intelligence pervading the universe and affecting its course. Psychic consciousness . . . an altered state of consciousness . . . as in sleep, hypnosis, meditation, and opening psychic doors. . . .

Much is said in this definition about "intelligent, invisible force." The premise of those who believe in psychic power is that God is not the "intelligent, invisible force" behind all creation and purpose. These people believe in "powers, forces, ancient masters, primordial forms of intelligence, etc. . . . ."

Anyone familiar with the Bible, however, knows there are only two sources of power in the universe, the power of God and the power of the fallen angel, Lucifer, known as Satan. If humans are not in contact with the powers or forces of God, that leaves only one alternative, the forces of evil.

From the beginning of time, it has been the nature of "the Evil One" to appear as attractive to humans as possible in order to work his deceptions. The book of Genesis recounts his first appearance to Eve in the Garden of Eden. The Bible tells us he took on the form of what, at that time, was the most beautiful creature in the Garden, a serpent. Through his wiles and half-truths he succeeded in deceiving Eve and subsequently Adam, bringing about the fall of all mankind into sin.

Satan has not changed his strategy in contemporary times because it worked so well the first time. If he can convince people that his power is a benevolent, beneficial force which can be harnessed for good and if he can make people believe that the power of his demons is really their own power "channeled" in the right way, then he has succeeded in another great deception. This is the message of the New Agers and the occult. Satan is not seen as evil, if even acknowledged at all.

Pokemon is teaching children how to traffic in a demonic world of wizardry and sorcery. Pokemon trains children in the black arts to use, trust, and manipulate spiritual forces that the Bible calls *demons*. Satan does not mind acting as though his power is subject to our control if ultimately he can *blind* us and *bind* us in spiritual darkness.

Pokemon may be simply children's entertainment to parents and their youngsters, an innocent dabbling in the fantasy world of the supernatural, but I assure you, Satan is the mastermind behind this hugely successful attempt to, again, deceive the innocent. While our children play his "games," Satan and his host of hell are not playing games. They are playing for keeps. And the prize is the eternity of our children.

Similarities: Dungeons & Dragons

Satan always begins with offering a bait. In this case, he offers children a fun-filled fantasy and diversion from reality. To parents, the attraction is an opportunity to occupy their children with a seemingly harmless activity, freeing them to focus on other business. In short, Pokemon has become an extremely popular and handy babysitter. However, as children enter into the Pokemon game, it is inevitable that they must participate in a role-playing world of fantasy.

Multitudes of children have grown older and out of the Pokemon marketing target type. But waiting for them is another sinister role-playing fantasy game that takes them still deeper into the world of the occult. It is one of the most popular games ever marketed for youngsters and teens: Dungeons & Dragons, or D & D.

D & D material states, "The battle rages on with only the sharpest and fastest thinkers going out ahead of the pack of hungry and fighting players as each scheme and plot against the others to survive."

The instructions on how to play Dungeons & Dragons are very clear regarding the sinister nature of this insidious "game" and makes no attempt to camouflage the demonic nature of the game's extremely occultic components.

Participants are forthrightly instructed that the "War Room" is in the *mind* of each player. It is there that they are taught to engage their opponents in fantasized battles. These increasingly brutal struggles not only pit players against other players, but the warriors must also go up against the elements, the environment, creatures from this world and from "other worlds." The player must go into battle against gods, demons, devils, curses, and the powers of witchcraft. Every player is given instructions on how to *conjure* up all kinds of spirits, powers, and demonic entities to fight.

The complex rules of engagement explain how the outcome

of various parts of the game are contingent upon the extent to which a given player can expand existing limitations of his mind. All the rules, regulations, and an explanation of the *tools* available to the player are contained in a number of different D & D manuals, as well as volumes of books, with virtually hundreds of pages. Reading and understanding these governing aspects of the game is no simple task. The overriding challenge is not only to win the game, but also to stay alive.

D & D is one of the most complicated games on the market. The game begins as the Dungeon Master (DM) or god, sets the stage in the fantasy world. Each player then assumes the identity of the character he creates. This particular character is then assigned six basic abilities: strength, intelligence, wisdom, constitution, dexterity, and charisma. The guidelines given in the manual makes the determination of whether the character will be "good" or "evil."

The object of the game is to maneuver these characters through a maze of dungeons (tunnels) that are filled with monsters, magic, ambushes, and other high-risk adventures in a search for hidden treasures. In order for a player to survive, he is given special *helps,* such as magical weapons, potions, spells, and magical trinkets (i.e.: holy water, garlic, wolves' bones, etc.). They are also given more conventional weapons: daggers, hand axes, swords, and battle axes.

One of the most remarkable rules in D & D is that a player can stay in the game as long as his character is not eliminated by being killed. This means a player can play for a few hours or even years, as many do.

Players who continue in the game over an extended period of time begin to identify themselves with their character and all of his traits. For the vast majority of young people involved in D & D, the line separating reality from fantasy begins to grow fuzzy.

One authority familiar with the game and its negative consequences upon players said, "The stuff that makes me nervous is this over-identification with the characters. I've seen kids go into raging fits, scream for hours, and throw objects in anger when they lose a battle or when their character dies."

There are a growing number of critics, individuals, and groups who point out the adverse negative affects of the game and demonstrate how D & D promotes a remarkable amount of violence, teaches participants to subscribe to false religions, encourages sexual perversion, indoctrinates its players into witchcraft, and has been known to lead to crime, violence, rape, sexual abuse, suicide, and murder.

We have already shared the testimony of death row inmate Sean Sellers, who attributes his involvement in the occult and, ultimately, the murder of his parents to his participation in Dungeons & Dragons.

An Honest Evaluation

It is a wise parent who perceives that every activity they allow their children to participate in will be, on some level and to some degree, a learning experience. Parents may innocently allow their child to play Pokemon games or view the Pokemon programs, but the influences will still impact these children. They are drawn into the fantasy and ultimately will become involved as an acting participant. Loving parents must be put on notice that the addictive nature of role-playing fantasy games like Pokemon creates an appetite for more of the same, only on a deeper and expanded level.

D & D is providing the "next level" for children who have had their appetites whetted by Digimon and Pokemon. The similarities between all of these role-playing fantasy games are obvious and undeniable. The precepts and concepts of one are shared by all.

The Logos Christian Resource Pages, an online ministry of Logos Communication Consortium, Inc., recently distributed an exposé on D & D that reveals the true nature of many of these diabolic *games*. They write:

Promotion of Violence

. . . The following documented incidents occurred to D & D players as an apparent result of the game. In November '99, a twelve-year-old boy shot his brother. In January, a four-teen-year-old boy walked into school and killed a teacher. Psychiatrist Lawrence Johnson cautions, "If I had a child who tended towards schizophrenia, I'd never let him near D & D. There's a danger that it would reinforce feelings of grandiosity of omnipotence. Reality and fantasy are hard enough for schizophrenics to differentiate. . . ."

I must add here that reality and fantasy are not only hard for schizophrenics to differentiate, they are extremely difficult for children to differentiate as well. Parents must constantly strive to teach their children how to tell the difference between fantasy and reality rather than to facilitate their confusion by allowing them to be fed a steady diet of deception via Pokemon and like programs.

The analysis of D & D by Logos continues . . .

On Becoming A God

. . . The D & D manual states, "This game lets all your fantasies come true. This is a world where monsters, dragons, good and evil, high priests, fierce demons, and even the gods themselves may enter your character's life. . . .

"Whether or not the character activity professes [to worship] some deity, he or she will have an alignment and serve one or more deities" (from *Dungeon's Master Guide*, pg. 25).

Again, I want to point out how D & D creators have no aversion to exposing the pantheistic anti-Christian nature of this game. It is clarified for all participants that they will, willingly or unwillingly, serve a god or gods whether they want to or not. Further instruction teaches the assimilative powers of the characters to absorb the nature of these gods to whom they are aligned, thus becoming deities themselves.

Further comments on the D & D by Logos looks at the occultic nature of the game under . . .

Concerning Witchcraft/Demonology

. . . Swords and sorcery (witchcraft) best describes what this game is all about.

Another D & D guidebook states, "Magic users draw upon arcane powers in order to exercise their profession . . . He or she must memorize and prepare for the use of each spell and its casting makes it necessary to re-absorb the incantation by consulting the proper god of spells. . . ."

George Marsh, member of the Candova Mark School Board in California, states in a letter why he voted to remove D & D from the school district's summer program. "The Supreme Court already banned religious activity from public facilities. D & D is clearly religious in context."

Concerning Death

". . . If the assassination is being attempted by or on behalf of a player's character, a complete plan of how the deed is to be done should be prepared by the player involved and the precaution, if any, on the target character should be compared against the plan. Weapons damage always occurs and may kill the victim even though assassination failed" (*Dungeon Master's Guide*, pg. 75).

All of these role-playing fantasy games, D & D and Pokemon included, not only indoctrinate young minds with witchcraft and the occult, but they instruct children in the application of subjective values. In playing the games, children are taught that sometimes it is not only necessary to lie, cheat, poison, deceive, and murder, but in fact, preferred and commendable to do these things. No value is placed on correct moral judgement, life is not sacred, and the ends justify the means in the *game*.

The Logos evaluation of D & D continues with a look at the game's thought on . . .

Concerning Sexual Perversion

. . . "These evil creatures will expect to loot, pillage, and **rape** freely at every chance and then kill (and probably eat) their captives" (*Players Handbook,* pg. 31).

The game may be "just a game." However, it has become much more to many people. In Seattle, a father is under treatment because his son used his service revolver to kill himself after being involved in D & D for only two years. In January, a seventeen-year-old walked onto a school stage, pointed a sawed-off shotgun to his head, and fired. Many, many cases are on public record of involvement that D & D is leading to violence, murder, and suicide. . . .

Only A Game?

. . . Yes, it is only a game, but . . . we become what we think, according to Proverbs 23:7, "For as a man thinketh in his heart, so is he." Proverbs 4:23, "Keep thy heart with all diligence, for out of it are the issues of life."

If we dwell on rape, murder, demons, sadism, prostitution, and witchcraft (which are but a few of the preoccupations of D & D) we absorb that knowledge and that line between fantasy and reality is removed and may leave no way out but death. . . .

Chapter 6

Harry Potter Phenomena

The most amazing publishing phenomena of all time is the Harry Potter series. This story, revolving around the experiences of a fictional character named Harry Potter, is making an unprecedented favorable impact upon children worldwide for the occult.

Harry is an eleven-year-old boy who is a wizard. He uses his magical powers as he goes through life's experience in his quest to "do the right thing." The books are filled with intrigue, mystery, and heroism. Unfortunately, they are also filled with blatant demonstrations of witchcraft, occultic powers, violence, and all sorts of New Age teachings. Each book is a virtual graduate course for children on how to use "good magic" and how to manipulate spiritual powers to accomplish their ends.

The first three parts in the series have sold over thirty-three million books, an unprecedented retail achievement. The fourth installment was released at midnight on July 8, 2000. The event was covered by news agencies around the world, including ABC's "Nightline" program. All over the United States, tens of thousands of parents and children lined up at bookstores waiting the stroke of midnight for the book's release. Near riot conditions were reported in some locations as parents and their offspring scrambled to get their latest Harry Potter book. Most of the children, as well as parents, were wearing the costumes that their fictional hero, Harry Potter, the wizard, wears in the books. Most children also sported the lightning marks upon their foreheads, which the young wizard received as a result of an evil curse that was put upon him as a small child.

On the first run of this fourth book, the publishers printed an astounding five million copies. Another ten million copies were ordered immediately after the first run sold out. Amazon.Com, the Internet book sales company, witnessed the value of their Wall Street stock increase significantly, simply because of their massive sales of Harry Potter's fourth book.

Even a casual investigation of the book's content reveals anti-Christian and occultic themes throughout the series. And yet, it is the greatest literary rage in recorded history and making its way to the silver screen as movie makers rush to cash in on the Harry Potter craze.

The *New York Times* Best Seller List had all four Harry Potter books on its Top Ten features at one time. This previously unprecedented event forced the creation of an entirely new category which would list best-selling children's books on their own "best-selling list."

Children's psychologists, sociologists, and book critics everywhere are praising Harry Potter as a "wonderfully exciting literary revolution that is bringing millions of children back to the wonderful world of reading."

Tragically, these so-called critics are ignoring the dark occultic nature of Harry Potter and the impact that such an influence is going to have upon millions of children.

Again, we are witnessing a sociological rage that is opening the lives and homes of countless millions of parents and children to satanic influences of wizardry, mediumistic powers, and demonic activity. But, astonishingly, it's the parents who are leading the charge to get their children involved in the world of Harry Potter.

How tragic it is to witness these parents in their naiveté and ignorance eagerly introduce their children to entertainment that is a deadly trap that could end up literally destroying their lives.

The Wicked World of Harry Potter

The main reason I decided to write this book was to expose the sinister ideological roots from which the majority of children's programs and recreational activities are coming. Everything I have exposed concerning the intimate relationship between the occult/New Age and Pokemon is equally true about Harry Potter. If there is a difference, it would be in the fact that, as hard as it may be to believe, Harry Potter is much more aggressive in its seductive appeal to get children involved in witchcraft and the occult. This subtle evangelistic quality of Harry Potter is far more covert than overt in that children are drawn to emulate the heroic lifestyle of the story's central character, a wizard named Harry Potter.

In fact, this wildly popular series is the most mind–boggling illustration of the psycho-spiritual assault which America's children are now experiencing.

Author J. K. Rowling has succeeded at producing the kind of literary masterpieces that, according to contemporary critics, places her in the league of Shakespeare, Poe, and Mark Twain. These are pretty heady names with which to compare one's work, and yet the sales of her books far exceed the total number of works sold by the three other famous authors combined.

To date, the four books that comprise the series are, in the order of their release, *Harry Potter and the Prisoner of Azkaban,* of which critics from the *School Library Journal* said, "Isn't it reassuring that some things just get better and better? This is a fabulously entertaining read that will have Harry Potter fans cheering for more."

Harry Potter and the Chamber of Secrets was acclaimed by a glowing review from *Booklist* which wrote:

Harry Potter's exploits during his second year at Hogwarts School For Witchcraft and Wizardry completely lived up to the bewitching measure. . . . The mystery, zany humor, student rivalry, and eccentric faculty are as expertly crafted as the heroes as in the first book.

Harry Potter and the Sorcerer's Stove received rave reviews by the *Boston Globe* and the *New York Times Book Review,* which wrote repeatedly, "A charming, imaginative, magical confection of a novel," and, "Funny, moving, and impressive."

Published by Arthur A. Levine Books, the Harry Potter series continues to break national and international sales records, enriching both the publishers and its author.

More Darkness

The insatiable appetite of young children for things spiritual is being fed and nurtured by the supernatural appeal of these Harry Potter books. In addition to the draw of the series' supernatural traits is the added alteration of its central character, eleven-year-old Harry.

Harry is a wizard who, along with a menagerie of other characters in the story, relies upon occultic powers to achieve his goals and overcome obstacles. Unlike many children's games, programs, and movies of the past in which the occultic and New Age agenda and philosophies are totally or partially camouflaged, the Harry Potter series is boastfully bold in the demonstration and flaunting of its dark and demonic content.

This in-your-face audacious demonstration of witchcraft, complete with its message of situation ethics and anti-Christian themes, has not only failed to hinder its popularity but rather boosted it. In fact, the flagrant and no-holds-barred occultic theme that drives the entire Harry Potter series is one of the most, according to secular observers and critics, stimulating facets of its commercial appeal.

One would think that a dark, demonic, and evil story filled with witchcraft, death, and wicked characters who cast spells and kill opponents to accomplish their goals, would not be the kind of literature that parents would want their children to consume. And yet, clearly it appears that the opposite is true. Not only are parents purchasing these books for their children, ages six to sixteen, but are themselves devouring the writings of J. K. Rawlings.

In my ministry of almost thirty years, I cannot remember any book or series of books receiving the kind of positive acclaim and praise for the secular community as has Harry Potter.

To demonstrate the hysteria that is sweeping the globe over this children's series, I want to insert a recent book review. I have taken the liberty of italicizing various phrases, words, and names that indicate those elements or characteristics associated with the series which clearly demonstrate the occultic, New Age, and satanic nature and theme of this diabolic literary phenomena.

The following book review was published in numerous newspapers, including the *Houston Chronicle*, the week of July 8–16, 2000. The italicization of words, again, is done by this author to illustrate the dark nature of the series and to highlight anti-Christian elements associated with it.

Book Review By Jane P. Marshall
New Potter Book Is the Best of the Bunch

Oops! She did it again.

J. K. Rowling's latest adventure featuring young *wizard* Harry Potter has been more eagerly anticipated than the identity of the sole surviving Survivor (on TV's real life drama by the same name.)

Not since the Beatles has Great Britain produced such an object of desire.

Does the two and a half pound *Harry Potter and The Goblet of Fire* . . . justify the eagerness factor? Is it *dark* and *virulent* as rumored? Has Rowling lost her touch as she has gained fortune — a reported fifteen million dollars in all — and fame?

Verdict: [Her fourth and latest installment of Harry Potter] *Goblet* is the best yet.

Tale number four is less lighthearted than the first thrills, but then fourteen is a serious age, especially when you are a marked *young wizard*.

Forget the comparison to Lewis Carroll and J. R. R. Tolkien. Harry Potter #4 puts Rowling in the same creative league as *Star Wars* creator George Lucas, and *X-Files* guru Chris Carter. Her *evil* characters make Darth Vader seem like Tinkerbell. Her *magic spells* could inspire another seven seasons of *X-Files*.

Goblet begins with a scene sinister enough to make Edgar Allen Poe proud. The *evil Lord Voldemort* is back, determined to re-establish his *reign of terror*.

His main obstacle is Harry Potter, the orphaned *wizard*.

Harry and his friends get tickets to the final match of the 422nd Quidditch World Cup. . . .

The match between Bulgaria and Ireland has all the pageantry and hope of an NBA play-off game: *spell-casting mascots*, marketing plays, *dirty tricks*, and distracted referees.

A *Dark Mask* appears in the sky, *striking horror* into the sports fans. The Mask, a trademark of Lord Voldemort, hasn't been seen for 13 years. It can only be *conjured* by *Death Enters*, the *Dark Lord's* supporters.

Why thirteen years? Harry is fourteen. When he was one, Valdemort tried *to do him in*, but failed. The confrontation left Harry with a *shiny, lightning-shaped scar* on his *forehead*, and Voldemort *without a body*. Voldemort's *trans mogrification* is one of the best scenes Rowling has ever written.

The story then moves to *Hogwarts School of Witchcraft and Wizardry*, where the headmaster announces the *Tri-Wizard Competition.*

Champions from three schools, chosen by another amazing Rowling creation called the *Goblet of Fire* will compete. . . .

. . . Other highlights of Goblet:

- A character dies. This isn't new, Rowling *kills off folks* now and then. But this character, no we're not telling who, is a good student. Rowling handles the *death* with an unusual combination of spunk. . . .
- Best new *magic*: Professor Dumbledores' trunk with seven locks. As each lock is opened, new contents are revealed.
- Best new character: the wonderfully crafted Alasoor "Madeye" Moody, *an Auro (dark wizard catcher)* with a magic eye that moves around his head so that he can see everything. He teaches *Dark Arts* at Hogwarts. . . .

. . . Will children read the two-inch thrill book? Of course they will. They'll sling it in their backpacks and take it to camp, too. Young Potter fans are loyalists. A mere 734 pages cannot come between them and their hero.

Should they read it, *this edgy tale with murder, torture, and evil oozing from every chapter?*

Of course! If they are old enough to take the physical Rowling challenge and heft the book, then they are old enough for the mental challenge.

. . . *Goblet of Fire* beautifully sets up the continuing saga of Harry, for whom Rowling has three more books planned.

Hang on to your . . . *[magic] wand.* The ride has just begun.

As you can see, this simple but rather sensationalized review of Harry Potter part four is full of words, phrases, and terminology that reveal the demonic and anti-Christian nature of the entire Potter series.

It is impossible for parents to ignore the profoundly apparent use of witchcraft, casting of spells, and occultic activities throughout the story. And make no mistake about it, the use of and reliance upon these satanic operations are not featured as the negative characteristics of evil characters in the story.

Like the theme of Pokemon, the Harry Potter stories are promoting and advocating the use of witchcraft by the heroes and heroines in the book. One need not be a theologian to understand that the advocated use of that which the Word of God forbids is a defiance of God Almighty and all that He stands for.

This chapter is not meant to be a thorough biblical critique of the Harry Potter writings. It is, however, intended to point out how insipidly audacious the proponents of the New Age, occult, and witchcraft have become in the marketing of their ideals and religions to the children of the world.

Loving parents who care about the future and the eternal destination of their children cannot ignore this ever–increasing spiritual assault that their children are undergoing in the world of children's games, programming, entertainment, and literature.

Contrast

The Scriptures are clear. No man or woman "can serve two masters, for he will love one and hate the other." Parents must not ignore the spiritual axiom that it is impossible for a child, or adult for that matter, to maintain an allegiance to two different authorities.

Christian parents who take their children to church and instruct them in the Scriptures, while simultaneously allowing them to participate in, read after, and play with activities, literature, and programs laced with the philosophies of the occult and witchcraft, are setting their children up for a catastrophic spiritual collision.

The spiritually polluted nature of stories like Harry Potter and games such as Pokemon, will grossly contaminate the values and moral foundations of any child. The teachings and philosophies that are woven into these children's attractions are spiritual poison and Christian parents have a God-given responsibility to forbid their children's participation in such things.

Harry Potter, for instance, teaches children how to manipulate demonic forces by the power of witchcraft. It teaches the child how to use God-forbidden techniques to accomplish objectives. The Word of God, however, teaches children how to live a life of faith and how to believe God to accomplish divine objectives.

Harry Potter trains children to rely upon the black arts and occultic powers. The Word of God trains children to trust in and place their full confidence in their Heavenly Father for all things.

Harry Potter justifies the use of evil to reach personal goals. God's Word equips children to know the difference between evil and righteousness. It demonstrates how righteousness and truth will ultimately triumph over evil.

Contrary to the philosophy espoused by Harry Potter, the Scriptures teach children that right is always right and that wrong is always wrong and that it is never right to do wrong.

Harry Potter, by repeated inferences and by the omission of spiritual facts, instructs its readers to ignore the reality of a personal God. Harry Potter's world is a world where no one needs to be concerned about the consequences of their sin and rebellion against a holy God. In Harry's world, the only deity one needs to be aware of or accountable to is self. Self-actualization and self-service are the goals of the individual and, therefore, one need not concern themselves with any future accountability to the God of the universe.

In Harry's world, there are supernatural forces and deities, but they can be manipulated to serve the will of a wizard master. In the real world, created by Jehovah God, people are not the manipulators of spirits, forces, and little gods. People, in the real world were created by the Father for the purpose of knowing and loving Him. In that relationship, which comes through knowing His Son, Jesus Christ, man discovers life by submitting to God, not manipulating Him.

Harry's world is one of darkness, deception, and treachery, where evil is praised and wickedness is rewarded. In that world, children learn to trust satanic forces and to fellowship with demons.

Yes, these malevolent entities and activities are camouflaged behind a veil of good intentions and innocent fun. But, sooner or later, all who enter the world of Harry Potter must meet the true face behind the veil. And when they do, they discover what all those who toy with evil discover, and that is, that while they may have been just playing, the Devil always plays for keeps.

Chapter 7

Opened Eyes

Every parent must learn to keep their spiritual eyes open for the deceptive tactics of the spiritual forces that are targeting their children. Therefore, it is imperative that parents educate themselves regarding the spiritual nature of the world in which they are raising their children. The natural world in which we live is a mere reflection of the spirit world and there are numerous parallele realities.

For instance, a key component to the physical development, health, and maturity of children is food. Few parents I know would allow their children to exclusively indulge themselves in junk foods, candy, and soda pop at every meal. The results for such a child would be a catastrophic physical condition. Conversely speaking, parents must not allow their children to gorge their minds with spiritual junk foods.

Unfortunately, most parents in our society remain uninformed concerning spiritual realities. Children must be guided by informed parents in their television viewing and entertainment habits. Even the most spiritually-minded and conscientious parents must remember that hardly a day goes by when their children are not exposed to the subtle influences of the New Age movement, the occult, or Satanism. The truth is, these satanic influences are behind the vast majority of the conflicts our children face.

However, just realizing our children are growing up in a world of spiritual warfare is not enough. Because of the growing intensity of this warfare, we as parents must give ourselves time to study and to stay informed about how to counteract these diabolic attacks upon our kids.

Just as God entrusted children to parents expecting them to feed and protect them physically, He has also entrusted parents with the spiritual nurturing of their children. Vigilance in parental efforts to know the messages woven into and often hidden in the programs and games our children participate in is an absolute essential. Learn to think critically, to focus on the dialogue of cartoon characters, and to listen for key words and phrases that are part of the scripts.

The Saturday morning when I walked in on my son as he watched the Pokemon cartoon was not, for me, a convenient moment to focus on the program's content and to attempt a character analysis. As I have already mentioned, I am not a "morning person." My body may be moving in the pre-dawn hours, but my intellectual and analytical capabilities are still dead to the world. However, because I have trained myself to listen to what is being said "between the lines" in children's programming and to discern the spiritual connotations of the plots, I made it a point, when I came out of my coma later in the morning, to pursue my investigation of Pokemon.

Procrastination in looking into the spiritual diet that our children are consuming in the programming they watch has extremely negative consequences. As parents, we will either facilitate the efforts of these forces who are out to enslave our children, or we will involve ourselves and frustrate the well-laid plans of these godless influences.

Once a parent has become informed about the nature of various negative influences and demonic content that inundates children's programming they must then develop a definitive strategy to protect their children and to provide fun-filled, stimulating alternatives.

Knowing the Spirits

Increasingly over the last several decades, consumers in America have learned how to become more health conscious than in previous years. As I was growing up, I cannot remember ever going to the grocery store with my mother and seeing a shopper reading the ingredients on the packages. However, the vast majority of people in our country have become *label readers,* as they want to be sure that what they are putting in their bodies is not going to clog their arteries, does not contain too much fat, or is not lacking in essential vitamins.

If parents were as concerned about the spiritual content of what their family is consuming as they are of the physical, new demands would be placed upon the creators of children's programming.

Christian parents have a biblical mandate to "test the spirits" behind the messages that are being absorbed by their children's minds. The epistle of First John in chapter four, verse one, states, "Beloved, believe not every spirit, but try the spirits whether they are of God; because many false prophets are gone out into the world." While certainly we should be concerned about false preachers in our pulpits, it is equally important that parents understand the evangelistic nature of those who are creating occultic New Age children's entertainment.

Under no circumstances am I espousing that we as parents are to live in fear of these demonic forces who are busily ministering to America's children. The Bible teaches us not only to be alert to these deceptive activities, but to have no fear of them. God's Word states, ". . . greater is he who is in you, than he that is in the world" (1 John 4:4).

God simply demands that we realize there is a great spiritual warfare being waged to spiritually deceive and ensnare people. And, yes, even Christians are targeted by these demonic forces. Paul writes in Ephesians 6:12, "For we wrestle not against flesh and blood, but against principalities, against powers, against the rulers of the darkness of this world, against spiritual wickedness in high places."

Failure to acknowledge these biblical truths and to enter into this warfare equipped with the full armor of God will result in horrendous spiritual defeats in a Christian's life. For Christian mothers and fathers who fail to wage this warfare against the host of hell, whose aim is to spiritually enslave their children, the results can be heartbreaking.

Unfortunately, most parents walk in great spiritual darkness not realizing how naive they are to the scriptural truths regarding this universal assault. Tragically, they and their children are, by the multiplied millions, falling into the diabolic ambush of satanic influences.

Parents are tempted to consider it all "innocent" fun and games, and are seduced into placing little or no restraints on their children's viewing and reading habits. They literally march into what Second Timothy 2:26 calls "the snare of the devil."

The Snare

Our children are being raised in a culture that from the day of their birth is attempting to mold their thinking into compatibility with itself. God's Word instructs Christians to stand constant guard over their own lives as well as the lives of their children.

The apostle Paul wrote, "Beware lest any man spoil you through philosophy and vain deceit, after the tradition of men, after the rudiments of the world, and not after Christ" (Col. 2:8). It is this "philosophy" of which I warn parents. It is a philosophy that permeates the vast majority of children's entertainment today. Simply put, this "philosophy" attempts to answer life's questions and solve life's problems without involving the truth of the living God in the equation.

Any and all attempts to bring resolution to the universal mysteries that have forever plagued mankind without considering the absolute answers given by divine revelation in the Word of God can only result in great deception. Hence, the greatest philosophers of this century have no more "philosophical" *understanding* than do uncivilized heathens sitting around their campfires under a starry canopy. They are both ignorant of biblical truth.

Parents must understand that their children will, just as they have, someday ask the great questions, "Who am I? Why am I here? Where am I going?"

The only satisfactory, fulfilling, and honest answers to such questions are found in the Word of God. However, the great Enemy of Truth who began his rebellion as an angelic being, Lucifer, wants children to deny the divine realities of God's Word. What better way to deceive them with lies about God, eternity, salvation, and their purpose in life than to, at an early age, fill their minds and hearts with the idea that they are here to become a master of demon spirits, as is the message of Pokemon?

This Bible verse warning, "Beware lest any man spoil you," literally means, "Be very careful lest any man make a prey of you and capture you with his false beliefs." The ancient philosophy of the Greeks, the Romans, and even modern philosophy offers absolutely no answers or help to mankind in his spiritual quest. The philosophies of the New Age, the occultists, the Satanists, and the Wiccans all have their roots in the same dark soil of human and demonic reasoning. They promote ways of thought and lifestyles that choose against the divine truths of God's Word.

We as parents, especially Christian parents, cannot lightly regard the indoctrination of our children by the high-tech wizardry of today's true televangelists, the purveyors of philosophical darkness who write and produce the "vain deceit" that fills so much children's programming. Do not be deceived into believing that your church-attending child can remain unaffected by the seductive lure of these occultic forces. The demonic, dark world of Pokemon and a vast host of other children's entertainment offers your children nothing but lies, deception, and philosophical death. It trains the child to disregard the true and living God and to dabble and traffic in a world of demon spirits.

Yes, characters in these programs are cute, cuddly, and often irresistibly huggable. However, encouraging a child to embrace such entities and to put these "monsters in their pockets" is not too different than encouraging them to embrace and pocket rattlesnakes. The only difference is that one is poisonous to the body while the other is poisonous to the spirit.

Divine Direction

Throughout the Word of God Christians are given repeated warnings about participating in occultic activity.

It is appalling to me how many Christian parents have contacted us over the years asking questions about various children's cartoons and programs that are very clearly based on occultic/New Age story lines and characters. It has been pointed out in a previous chapter how many occultic, New Age, and satanic facets are obviously in Pokemon programming. Scripture clearly warns believers to refrain from involvement in and toleration of any of these kinds of activities.

Channeling

One of the most commonly used techniques recurring on the Pokemon program is the channeling of powers and *evolved* personalities. Channeling is a New Age term describing the use of one's body to transmit a message or power. In truth, it is the opening of one's physical body to demonic spirits in order for them to communicate a message.

In the Old Testament book of First Samuel we read where the king of Israel, Saul, consulted a witch in order to contact the dead prophet, Samuel. This was in direct contradiction to God's command and it cost Saul his life.

The Bible says in Leviticus 20:27, "A man also or woman that hath a familiar spirit . . . shall surely be put to death." God was extremely serious in his demand for spiritual purity because of the deceptive nature behind such occultic involvement. People are not to open their bodies to be used as highways for demonic commuters attempting to access the physical realm.

Wizards and Mediums

Should we allow our children to be entertained by wizards and those entities who claim to have all kinds of psychic powers, like so many of the little "pocket monsters" on Pokemon? God clearly answers the question in Leviticus 19:31, "Regard not them that have familiar spirits, neither seek after wizards, to be defiled by them; I am the Lord your God." God wants to protect us from the demonic defilement that comes from entertaining ourselves with these demonic entities.

Crystals, Magic Cards, Dreamers . . .

Pokemon is full of creatures pictured in the multitudes of powerful Pokemon trading cards that use power-filled stones, who steal dreams, and move *forces*. God's Word also addresses these characters and their powers in Deuteronomy 13:1–3:

> If there arise among you a prophet, or a dreamer of dreams, and giveth thee a sign or a wonder, and the sign or the wonder come to pass, whereof he spake unto thee, saying, Let us go after other gods, which thou hast not known, and let us serve them; Thou shalt not hearken unto the words of that prophet, or that dreamer of dreams: for the Lord your God

proveth you, to know whether ye love the Lord your God with all your heart and with all your soul.

New Age Teachings

The fundamental doctrine of New Agers that humans can interpose themselves into a cosmic force and use powers to gain god-like qualities is clearly addressed in the Word of God. Paul wrote of such people in the New Testament book of Romans, chapter one, where he says of them in verse twenty-five, "Who changed the truth of God for a lie, and worshiped and served the creature more than the Creator. . . ."

Supernatural Feats

Pokemon of various kinds demonstrate numerous powers that help them defeat, poison, destroy, and overcome their opponents. These powers range from employing the elements, as do witches, to divination and psychic phenomena, all forbidden in Scripture.

The Bible states in Deuteronomy 18:10–12:

> There shall not be found among you anyone who maketh his son or his daughter to pass through the fire, or that useth divination, or an observer of times, or an enchanter, or a witch, Or a charmer, or a consulter with familiar spirits, or a wizard, or a necromancer. For all that do these things are an abomination unto the Lord; and because of these abominations the Lord thy God doth drive them out from before thee.

Saying "No"

Once a parent realizes how clearly God's Word speaks to this kind of issue, and once they understand the spiritual danger that Pokemon and other similar children's programs are to their child, it is necessary to take appropriate steps to intervene.

In the case of my own nine-year-old son, I decided to point out the obvious scriptural problems with the Pokemon story line and its demonic characters. Knowing that he had for years been taught to recognize the fingerprints of satanic programming and that in each case when previously confronted with a choice he had always made the right one, I wanted him to choose correctly on the Pokemon issue as well.

I have already explained how I began over a period of days to discuss with him the things I had found out about his favorite new cartoon, Pokemon. At first, he casually resisted my suggestion that it looked like Pokemon contained some very demonic characters. I must confess that when I began to see how absolutely devilish this stuff was that I wanted to jerk his GameBoy Pokemon out of his hand and forbid his involvement with the games, the cartoons, and the Pokemon movies.

However, I repeat, there comes a time when children must be taught the facts, be challenged to act, and then given the opportunity to make the right choice. Of course, if they fail to choose correctly, ultimately, parents must move to intervene.

So I prayed for God to give my son wisdom, I fed him the right information telling him what the Word of God said, and then watched as over the next several days he became more and more uncomfortable with his Pokemon game and program.

Finally, one day I came home and asked my wife, Suzanne, where Philip was. She responded, "I don't know. He just grabbed a hammer and went out to the backyard a little while ago."

Suddenly I heard an explosive, "BANG! BANG! BANG!" that caused me to run to the window overlooking the back porch. There I saw my son, Philip, on the porch, with all sixty-five pounds of his 5'4" frame, being thrown into the process of smashing his beloved Pokemon game into a thousand pieces with the hammer. He was obviously not content to simply break it. He clearly wanted it totally obliterated. He then meticulously picked up as many of the tiny pieces as possible and with them cupped in his little hands, started towards the backdoor.

I quickly ran over and sat down on the couch, picked up a book, and tried to look as casual as possible. Philip then burst in the back door and walked straight to the couch. With a wide and proud smile on his face he cunningly said, "Hey Dad! Wanna play Pokemon? Too bad, 'cause you'll have to fix it!"

Then, his eyes alight with glee, he held his cupped hands over my lap and slowly, with the greatest deliberation, let the thousands of tiny Pokemon pieces rain from his hands.

I looked into his eyes with a Dad's very grateful heart and with my greatest exuberance told him how thankful I was to have such a smart son, one who knew how to make brave, hard, tough decisions in order to stand up for what is right.

He strutted for days.

Over the next few days I looked for ways to bless his obedience and to reward his right choices.

But children and young people can only make the right decision and correct choices in life if someone is equipping them with the right information and challenging them with the clear truths of God's Word. It is up to parents to teach themselves and then to teach their children to make the God-honoring decision that will put a hedge of God's truth around their lives and protect their futures.

Chapter 8

Refocusing

A remarkable number of parents have written our ministry reflecting the same concerns as those I received from the distraught parents who wrote:

> ... Since the Pokemon craze swept into the lives of our children our home life has radically changed. Our three children have increasingly withdrawn from family life to focus on playing Pokemon. They have lost all interest in home life, in their schoolwork, and in spending time with us, their parents. All they want to do is play Pokemon.

Multitudes of parents are witnessing the same kind of evolution in their children's behavior since Pokemon was introduced into their homes.

I want to briefly reiterate that the role-playing nature of the Pokemon game blurs the line between the real world and the fantasy world in the minds of children. It also teaches them to accept otherwise forbidden activities as normal and acceptable. The message ultimately incorporated into the child's thinking is: "In order to achieve your goals, it is just fine to poison, injure, cheat, kill, and deceive." This is the philosophy that is in direct contradiction to the message that Christian parents are struggling to ingrain in their children: the ends never justify the means.

Pokemon conditions children through a process of penalties and rewards to "win at all costs." The game rewards children with a euphoria, a psychological high for winning. This facet of the game explains the psychological addiction that many parents are noticing. This addiction compels children to spend as much time as possible with their Pokemon paraphernalia, at the expense of other recreation, time with their families, and attention to schoolwork.

This craving for more and more Pokemon involvement is nothing short of manipulation by the Pokemon creators and marketers. And yet, because many parents are just too busy to get involved and are so trusting of this godless system, they have no idea what is happening to their children.

Pokemon is really only the tip of a very large iceberg. Children's minds and lives are being corrupted and consumed by satanic forces through the media of children's television, entertainment, music, and even the Internet at an unprecedented rate. Nor can anyone deny the overwhelming powerful impact that children's literature, like Harry Potter, is having on millions of children worldwide.

One of the latest national polls reveals that children between the ages of two and eighteen years spend almost five and a half hours every day watching television. The poll also showed that fifty-three percent of America's children have a television in their bedroom, seventy percent have a radio as well in the same bedroom, and sixty percent watch television during every meal. Almost fifty percent of the families surveyed said, "We have no TV rules" for what is viewed in the home.

So much of this interaction between kids and TV takes place in their own bedrooms without the slightest amount of parental supervision. To allow a child to have a TV in their bedroom is like inviting a babysitter you've never met and without trusted references to guard your child for hours on end. The results are often devastating.

Deciding To Act

The option before parents today is simple. They can stay uninvolved with their children's recreational habits and witness the eventual destruction of their children's lives or they can decide to educate themselves and move to save their children untold heartache in the future.

Many parents might say, "But I'm not sure how to teach my children what's good or bad programming and activities." For that, however, God has given us a clear and practical example in the way that He has dealt with His children from the very beginning of creation. In Genesis, chapter three, God put Adam and Eve in a virtual paradise. Upon instructing them regarding conduct, He first emphasized all the positive and exciting opportunities and experiences that were available to them in the Garden. He showed them all of the thousands of great choices they had before them in things to experience, to touch, and to eat.

Finally, he pointed to the single item in the Garden that He forbade them to eat. With absolute clarity He warned, "For in the day ye eat thereof ye shall surely die." God did not want Adam and Eve, and consequently the entire human race and nature itself, to experience the fall that their disobedience would bring about, so He warned them of the consequences.

I have often heard parents say, "Well, I believe in the school of hard knocks. Kids learn by their mistakes." That is a foolish position for any parent to take. It reveals deep spiritual ignorance and a lack of personal discipline.

While certainly we all ought to learn from our mistakes, it is much wiser to learn from the mistakes of others. Then we do not have to bear the scars of the failures. God intended for Adam and Eve to learn about evil, not through personal experience, but rather by discerning it as something vile, destructive, and totally foreign to the Holy Spirit which was to guide their lives.

Parents, our kids will fail, but we can protect them from the great failures that are ruining the lives of so many millions of young people today by biblical instruction, vigilant discipline, and personal involvement.

Truths to Teach Children

I want to suggest five things that every parent should begin instilling into the thinking of their children at the earliest age possible. These five principles will give children a foundation upon which to learn to think for themselves. They will also provide parents with a foundation upon which to build further instruction with greater truths.

1) Emphasize God's goodness and sin's penalties.

Parents must primarily instill in their children that there are consequences for all behavior. Children must learn that God is a rewarder of those who diligently seek him (Heb. 11:6). Conversely, they must also be taught that choosing to disobey and to rebel brings with it a penalty.

For parents who have been raised on the philosophy of Dr. Spock, who feels that discipline is anathema, this may be a difficult premise to receive. However, God's Word is clear that "foolishness is bound in the heart of a child, but the rod of correction shall drive it far from him" (Prov. 22:15). Parents must learn the principles of biblical discipline and apply them, understanding the difference between loving discipline and child abuse.

In applying the system of rewards and penalties, parents are reinforcing on each occasion the fact that there is a right and a wrong. We must be absolutely certain that a child's understanding of right is connected with "thus says the Lord," not "thus says Mommy or Daddy."

When children ask that inevitable question of, "Why can't I?" parents must not simply say, "Because I said so." They

A Fatal Attraction — 99

should rather point to the higher authority of God's Word.

Obedience must be noticed, noted, and praised. Disobedience must also be noticed and the application of appropriate penalties must be swift.

2) Teach your child to stand against evil and injustice.

The Bible says, "And have no fellowship with the unfruitful works of darkness, but rather reprove them" (Eph. 5:11).

Christians should aggressively instruct their children to speak out against wrong, evil, and injustice when they encounter it. My children have often reported to me over the years instances when they have confronted their playmates or friends on questionable issues. Speaking out in such a way does quite often bring ridicule upon a child. Yet, a parent must use these occasions to instruct their children that people who stand up for truth will often be persecuted. Paul writes in Second Timothy 3:12 that all who live godly will suffer persecution.

However, it is this kind of persecution that builds character in children and young people, reinforcing in their psyche that they, indeed, are doing the right thing.

3) Teach your child that Satan controls this world's systems.

Every parent should instill in their children the biblical truth that the philosophies that will bombard them via most secular music, literature, media, education, and entertainment is born of an anti-Christ spirit. Therefore, they must learn from discerning parents how to recognize evil even when it comes in subtle and attractive packages.

As previously mentioned, children must be taught that there is a "lying spirit" out to corrupt, deceive, and destroy their lives. Teaching a child how to think critically about everything he is exposed to will insure his future spiritual protection.

Learning to recognize the messages buried in the story

lines, lyrics, plots, characters, and agendas of those with whom they interact daily is an imperative. Children must be taught that there are malevolent forces out to convince them to reject the fundamental doctrines and truths of God's Word.

4) Teach your children to know and to observe God's standards and ways.

God expects, yea, He demands that parents raise their children in the "nurture and admonition of the Lord" (Eph. 6:4).

In the Old Testament book of Deuteronomy, God emphasizes how vital early and consistent biblical training must be. Deuteronomy 6:6–9 says:

> And these words, which I command thee this day, shall be in thine heart: and thou shalt teach them diligently unto thy children, and shalt talk of them when thou sittest in thine house, and when thou walkest by the way, and when thou liest down, and when thou risest up. And thou shalt bind them for a sign upon thine hand, and they shall be as frontlets between thine eyes. And thou shalt write them upon the posts of thy house, and on thy gates.

In the Old Testament culture, godly parents were vigilant to never allow the pagan to "touch the palate" of their children. It is said that the *taste* that touches the palate of a young child are those tastes that are preferred through the life of that child. This, simply put, means that Christian parents have a scriptural obligation to protect their children in their early developmental stages from cultural trends and philosophies that are popular with the pagan, yet forbidden by God. Parents must not allow a godless culture and influences to have access to their young children's sensitive minds and hearts. In these early years of maturation, children must be sheltered from the lying influences that dissuade them from God's truth. As children grow it is the parents responsibility to teach the child how to receive or reject the ideologies and philosophies that appeal to and influence his mind, body, and soul.

Parents who are serious about training their children in "the nurture and admonition of the Lord" must accept their assignment as the "watchmen of their children's soul." We, as parents, are to be the gatekeepers of all that enters into our children's minds and hearts, constantly filtering out the evil and pouring in the righteous.

Children must be taught from infancy the great truth of Philippians 4:8:

> Finally, brethren, whatsoever things are true, whatsoever things are honest, whatsoever things are just, whatsoever things are pure, whatsoever things are lovely, whatsoever things are of good report, if there be any virtue, and if there be any praise, think on these things.

5) Teach children to celebrate the fact that they are different.

Parents must early on instruct their children that as they surrender their lives and hearts to Christ they become "marked." The Bible calls this "marking of God" *sanctification.* This is no holier-than-thou expression, but a word that identifies every believer as one who has been "set aside by God for a special purpose."

This *specialness* means that each believer has an exciting, unique, and special call upon their life.

One Bible teacher I heard put it this way: "Every child comes into this world with a set of sealed orders. Part of the responsibility of Christian parents is to help their child unseal those orders."

To meet this challenge, parents must teach children to celebrate this difference from the world. They are not allowed to participate in some activities, go some places, and watch some programs because they are *different* from those whose parents have chosen not to follow Christ. This *separation* from the world, mandated by the Word of God, however, should be viewed by them as a privilege and part of their special heritage.

The Bible says of the children of God: "But ye are a chosen generation, a royal priesthood, an holy nation, a peculiar people, that ye should shew forth the praises of him who hath called you out of darkness into his marvelous light" (1 Peter 2:9).

As parents instill into their children the exciting truth that they are chosen of God, selected for royalty, and set aside for a divine destiny, then they get excited about participating in the process of their own spiritual development. A vital part of this training is for parents to find other Christian families with children the ages of their own who share these convictions.

Remember, parents are preparing their children for the call of God upon their lives. This takes vigilance, discipline, and training. If a child is to be what God wants them to become, they must be coached by godly parents.

I remember reading the story of the 1968 Olympic swimming champion Mark Spitz. His story is not unlike that of most champions and winners. A reporter asked him how he managed to win eight gold medals in one Olympics. Mark Spitz said: "I'm focused. I spend eight hours a day, seven days a week, doing nothing but swimming. While my friends and even some other contestants are out dating, partying, or goofing off, I swim."

This kind of consecrated discipline in the development of our children is a must. As parents remain focused on the goal of training their child to be a champion for Christ, there will be times when the child demands to know why they are not allowed to do what most other children are doing. These are the moments when parents must seize the opportunity to say,

"Oh, but son, you're not like other children. You belong to God and He has a greater call upon you. In order to fulfill it and to be all He wants you to be you must say 'no' to some things that others are saying 'yes' to."

But, parents must also strive to provide fun-filled alternatives to attractions like Pokemon and popular books like Harry Potter. Again, godly families with children around the same age can help immensely in this area as parents share their ideas and resources on providing wholesome, godly recreation for their children.

I beseech parents to constantly bring to remembrance, for their own benefit, that they have a divine appointment in the training of their children. And the Christian parent must sincerely commit to the uniqueness of God's call and demands upon them as well.

I sincerely believe that it would greatly benefit every parent to study the great Old Testament principle, borne out repeatedly in the New Testament, that God is working to set aside a special group of people to accomplish His purposes in this generation. This great truth is clearly stated in Deuteronomy 7:1-9:

When the Lord thy God shall bring thee into the land whither thou goest to possess it, and hath cast out many nations before thee, the Hittites, and the Girgashites, and the Amorites, and the Canaanites, and the Perizzites, and the Hivites, and the Jebusites, seven nations greater and mightier than thou; And when the Lord thy God shall deliver them before thee; thou shalt smite them, and utterly destroy them; thou shalt make no covenant with them, nor shew mercy unto them. Neither shalt thou make marriages with them; thy daughter thou shalt not give unto his son, nor his daughter shalt thou take unto thy son. For they will turn away thy son from following me, that they may serve other gods: so will the anger of the Lord be kindled against you, and destroy thee suddenly. But thus shall ye deal with them; ye shall destroy their altars, and break down their images, and cut down their groves, and burn their graven images with fire. For thou art an holy people unto the Lord thy God: the Lord thy God hath chosen thee to be a special people unto himself, above all people that are upon the face of the earth. The Lord did not set his love upon you, nor choose you, because ye were more in number than any people; for ye were the fewest of all people: But because the Lord loved you, and because he would keep the oath which he had sworn unto your fathers, hath the Lord brought you out with a mighty hand, and redeemed you out of the house of bondmen, from the hand of Pharaoh king of Egypt. Know, therefore that the Lord thy God, he is God, the faithful God, which keepeth covenant and mercy with them that love him and keep his commandments to a thousand generations. . . .

Chapter 9

Starting Right

As I have stated in previous chapters, parents have a God-given responsibility to protect their children from the seductive and satanic assault that they will surely experience. However, for even the most vigilant parents there will be those times when they are not around the child. I refer to those moments when a child is left with friends, family, or babysitters who may not share the parent's convictions. Add to this the many Christian parents who have their children in day-care centers or schools where the agenda is not controlled by the parent's convictions. Therefore, parents must learn how to set a hedge of God's protection around a child and trust God to do that which they cannot.

Parents must first understand the principle of stewardship. This is a term that means "one who is managing another's assets or materials." God has given parents the stewardship of their children and He entrusts their spiritual well-being to parental authority.

In fact, for years as the pastor in a local church I set aside several dates every year for the singular purpose of what we called "baby dedication." Parents of new babies who wanted to acknowledge God's ownership of their children would bring their child to the altar and there in front of the congregation would, through prayer and a vow of commitment, dedicate the child as well as themselves to God.

This act has no redemptive power as it pertains to the child's salvation. However, it was acknowledgement of the parents that they recognize their stewardship over the child and a commitment by them to raise that baby in the "nurture and admonition of the Lord."

On these special occasions I always read the Old Testament story of Hannah. Her story in First Samuel 1:1–28 is a precious picture of how God opened her closed womb after she sought God for this miracle. The result was the birth of a son named Samuel. In her pleadings to God to give her a son, she promised to give him back to God. In this beautiful story, that is exactly what Hannah does. At a certain point she goes to God and says, "So I have dedicated him to the Lord, as long as he lives he is dedicated to the Lord" (1 Sam. 1:28).

As parents publicly proclaim their decision to raise the child that God has given them stewardship over, they are not only making a statement to the congregation but they are also serving notice to the spiritual world. Satan is out to claim and corrupt everything that does not have the mark of God upon it. God has given Christian parents through repeated biblical precedents the right to claim their children for Christ. They are to do this understanding the imperative that they, as parents, are to live their lives in submission to God's call upon them.

Praying for a Child's Salvation

Though parents may dedicate their children to God at an early age this is only the beginning of a parent's prayer life for their children. This public dedication is to be followed up in the formulative years by consistent, reinforced teaching of the truths of God. But no matter how zealous a parent may be in their efforts to teach their child the vital importance of having a personal relationship with God through His Son, the Lord Jesus Christ, still each child must ultimately make their own decision to accept Christ as their Lord and Savior. So, parents must combine the instruction to their child with prayers for that child to come to a place where they will surrender their lives to Christ.

God has provided us with more than ample promises regarding His desire to answer to our prayers for the salvation of others, especially our own children. The Bible states in First John 5:14–15, "And this is the confidence that we have in him, that, if we ask anything according to his will, he heareth us: And if we know that he hear us, whatsoever we ask, we know that we have the petitions that we desired of him." These verses teach believers how critically important a part prayer plays in God's process of salvation. For years before our children received Christ as their personal Savior, my wife and I diligently and daily prayed for them to come to the place of full surrender to Him.

Binding the Strongman

Throughout the Word of God we see that Satan is working to blind hearts from understanding and receiving the graces of God. As already established, we live in a system that is working in harmony with these satanic efforts through countless ways. However, as parents work in the physical realm to forbid their children's participation in activities that give occultic and satanic influences access to their minds, they must also labor in the spiritual realm to protect their children. Because we "wrestle not against flesh and blood but against spiritual wickedness in high places," Christian parents must utilize spiritual weapons against satanic deception.

Just as we see the hedge of God around the life of Job in the Old Testament book of Job, we can see the hedge of God put around the lives of those we claim for the kingdom of God. Understanding that true prayer is prayer that originates with the Holy Spirit in the believer's life, parents must pursue the Holy Spirit-born burden to pray for their children's spiritual protection and ultimate salvation. It is God's Spirit which burdens the parent for the child. It is the parent who responds to the urgings of the Holy Spirit to agree with the Father for His will in the salvation of a child. God always answers the prayers that originate with Him.

Therefore, whether we understand the spiritual dynamics at work through the process of intercessory prayer or not, we can experience the glorious results of it by being faithful and diligent to pray daily for these two things: first, the protection of our children from lying, deceiving satanic influences, and second, for the salvation of our children when they reach an age of understanding.

Introducing Your Child to Christ

Parents who have been faithful to seek God's protection and leading for their children will eventually see their child come to the moment of decision regarding their acceptance of Christ as their personal Savior. On multitudes of occasions, I have had parents bring their children to my office when they felt their child was ready to make this life-changing decision. And on more occasions than I can count, a mother or father has walked into my office beaming with their smiling child and said, "Tell the pastor what happened to you this week." And then I would listen as the child told me in their own words how they had prayed with a sensitive parent to give their heart to Christ.

There will be a multitude of opportunities for a child raised in a home where Christ is Lord to come to know Christ as they reach the age, which varies with each child, when they are ready to choose Christ as their Lord and Savior. However, though parents know their child may have numerous places and opportunities to come to Christ, the parent must be constantly tuned to the spiritual frequency and temperature of their child's heart.

I have often heard of fathers who failed for various reasons to get their very pregnant wives to the hospital in time and were forced to participate in the birth of their own child. These fathers have a unique and life-changing experience as they play "midwife" at the birth of their own.

How much more unforgettable for a parent who encounters their child at that precise moment when the Holy Spirit wants to give birth to a new heart and life in their own child!

Parents should be ready for such an eventuality as children under the convicting power of the Holy Spirit will not wait for a convenient moment at church but want to settle the issue immediately. Answers should be made ready by parents who have children on the verge of making such a decision. A parent should be ready to confirm the child's need for Christ and be able to go over God's simple plan of salvation with a child. Praying out loud for and with a child who is ready to accept the Lord Jesus into their life is one of the most awe-inspiring and precious moments a parent can experience. That parent is acting as an agent of the Holy Spirit in a miraculous transition and such a moment is one that a parent and child will be able to share and cherish for all eternity.

Turning a Child from Evil

So many parents have come to me over the years explaining how their child, some Christian and some yet to accept Christ, have been involved in occultic/New Age/satanic games and activities but now want to renounce this involvement. Many with children involved in Pokemon and other such occultic-laced children's games and entertainment have witnessed terrible transformations in their children's personalities and behavior. I add this particular segment because many parents who read this book will identify with such a statement. Therefore, I want to provide concerned parents whose children are ready to forsake such satanic entrapments with a prayer that they may use as a model to pray with such a child.

I suggest that the parent first reinforce the biblical reasons why God wants His children to refuse participation in such games and recreation. Once a child's heart is pliable and made sensitive to obey the will and Word of God in this matter, then a parent may want to lead their child in the following prayer of repentance and commitment.

The parent should lead their child through such a prayer out loud:

Dear Heavenly Father, I come to you today asking for your forgiveness. I know that Your Word teaches us not to participate in, or to play with things that glorify Satan and his lying spirits. I do not understand many of the evil things that I have read, played with, and seen on TV, but I do know that these things do not honor and glorify the Lord Jesus Christ.

I do not want to be lied to or fooled by evil. I pray in the name of the Lord Jesus Christ that You, dear Father, would rebuke and bind all of Satan's evil influences away from my life. I plan to start obeying You right now. I surrender to do Your will in all areas of my life. Thank you, God, for loving me even when I sin. Now teach me, by the power of your Holy Spirit, how to love You more.

Affirming God's Truth to a Child

After going through such a prayer with any child, a parent needs to take a few moments at this special time to go over with the child some important, fundamental truths. These truths will minister great peace and assurance to any child while at the same time firmly establishing in their understanding the wonderful security they have in Christ.

I think it's fitting for a parent to read the following list, or one similar to it, out loud to the child and have the child affirm their commitment to each.

1. We believe that there is only one true God who is the Creator of all things that are.
2. We believe in the Lord Jesus Christ, God's only Son, who has overcome Satan and all evil.
3. We believe that the Lord Jesus Christ died on a cross as the payment for all sins because He loves us. He rose from the dead and now by His Spirit lives in our heart.
4. We believe that God has given us all power and authority over evil, Satan, and demons and we have no fear of them. As we stay obedient and strong in the Lord, God will protect us from all evil.
5. We believe that God wants us to fill our minds and hearts with good, pure, and right things, and to reject any and all involvement in occultic/New Age/ satanic recreation and entertainment.
6. We believe God has an exciting and thrill-filled life for us, His children, as we continue to seek to love and obey Him.

Parents who are willing to invest themselves in the spiritual protection and development of their children will reap a harvest of untold benefits. But the most profoundly rewarding benefit of all is watching a child grow up loving Christ with a divine sense of purpose and direction.

> I have no greater joy than to hear that my children walk in truth.
>
> — Third John 1:4

Chapter 10
In A Nutshell

We have examined how the subtle satanic influences in games like Pokemon and literature such as Harry Potter books can make them appear innocent. However, our examination of the facts have proven that this, and a vast number of other children's games and entertainment are like high diving boards from which children leap into a deep and dark pool of occultic deception.

It has also been established that Christian parents have a biblical mandate to keep their children from becoming involved in the kinds of activities promoted by Pokemon and Harry Potter such as magic, witchcraft, and seeking supernatural help or protection from power sources other than God.

I do not feel it's an overstatement based upon the facts we have shared in saying that the Pokemon games and the Harry Potter series' agenda, from a purely Christian prospective, is *sinister.*

When I first began to speak out on the Pokemon issue, I immediately began to receive letters from children and parents. A remarkable number in both of these groups were in essence saying, "But it's just a game!" My response to such reasoning is that Russian roulette is just a game as well. However, depending on the toys and tools used, games can become deadly serious.

The argument made by some parents is that their children do not take these games and books seriously. I remind them that there are demonic forces involved in these exchanges that do take these games very seriously. I add, God also takes it seriously when His people begin dabbling in the occult and trafficking in witchcraft. We have already looked at some of His severe warnings against such activities.

Stay Alert

Satan longs to ensnare children as young as possible. In fact, the Pokemon creators have released another game designed for children from the age of birth through five years old called Digimon. Digimon is based on the same occultic principles as Pokemon and also trains children in the art of becoming "masters." Remember the word "master" is yet another spin word for the New Age and the occult. The term "master" has its origins in Eastern-based religions and Zen Buddhism, and has application in the world of martial arts.

Caring parents should train themselves to know and recognize these spin words. My children recognize them as "giveaway terms" that expose occultic and New Age roots. Other words that ought to raise a red flag to parents are: *powers, power surge, focal points, telepathic, telemedic, summons, conjure, wizard, spells,* and *psychic links.* Parents should train their children that when the child hears these words used in a program, game, book, or cartoon to "come and tell Mommy or Daddy and we'll all examine the content together."

The Bait

Please note that as children begin to play the Pokemon game, they are permitted certain controls over various "pocket monsters" or demonic entities. This is to assist them in their quest to become masters. This *power* is a very seductive lure to young children.

The spiritualistic facet of the game is very attractive to children as well, and as they begin their quest it appeals not only to their natural curiosity about things supernatural but eventually to their egos as they discover that they can play a role in the manipulation of "monsters" and demons.

Their efforts, once they become more proficient at the game, are rewarded. This rewards system, based upon their performance, eventually leads to the psychological addiction referred to earlier. This addiction, like all addictions, cannot in itself sustain the psychological high, thus many children eventually get into even more sinister fantasy role-playing games. In fact, a number of Pokemon websites are very proud of their linkage with other fantasy role-playing games such as a very popular one among children and young teens called MAGIC. We have already pointed out the similarities between Pokemon and Dungeons & Dragons and Advanced Dungeons & Dragons.

Secular World Begins to See

I recently watched a major television network as they aired a special story on Pokemon "Pokemania." The special report featured pictures and interviews of children and parents who are caught up in this craze. The footage showed parents and their young ones in heated competition to gain more and more Pokemon creatures, Pokemon cards, and Pokemon paraphernalia. Parents were seen scrambling, shoving, and pushing each other as various retail outlets ran sales on different Pokemon products. Scuffles and arguments often broke out during these wild rampages as parents and children fought to secure the desired Pokemon products.

Footage was also shown of children who were arguing, fighting, screaming at one another, crying, and literally throwing tantrums in order to get their desired "pocket monster" trading cards. The report showed near riot conditions in some cases. The reporter summed up his piece by saying, "This is sheer Pokemon fanaticism, and for more and more parents they are witnessing their own children becoming more and more out of control."

Strangely these same conditions were replicated at the release of the fourth installment of the Harry Potter series. But on this occasion, millions of American's watched this phenomenal scramble to secure the book on television as virtually every major network in America had their news cameras and crews set up in bookstores across the country and around the world.

The Lessons

Pokemon and Harry Potter not only train children in the art of channeling demon spirits and powers through their bodies and minds, they also instruct them in the application of situation ethics. The satanistic doctrine that evil is good and good is evil is very much part of the Pokemon/Harry Potter philosophy. The goal orientation of the game and books repeatedly instills in young minds the idea that the ends, in fact, do justify the means.

So, we can add instruction in situation ethics to the Pokemon/Harry Potter curriculum along with their instruction in spiritism, lessons on how to kill, maim, and poison their opposition. These are not activities nor the sort of training that most parents, Christian or not, would want their children involved in.

Yes, I know the critics insist, "But it's only fantasy!" However, children are not skilled at discerning the difference between fantasy and reality. The truth is, this inability to distinguish between what is real versus what is not real is hardly restricted to children. A trip to one of America's many churches today would prove that millions of adults cannot tell the difference between the false and the real. In these churches, we are seeing satanic counterfeits of numerous spiritual gifts and miracles as undiscerning adults get caught up in a nationwide false revival.

But for children who are growing up participating in role-playing games and reading books where maiming, killing, poisoning, and eliminating opponents is normal and acceptable behavior, the line between fantasy and reality can get very blurred. It is not a very big step for many of these youngsters to go from blowing away their opponents on a screen with a controller to going on the streets and blowing away opposing gang members with a .357 revolver. They have to learn the hard way that in the real world victims do not just get up and walk away; they die.

Responding to Critics

After our initial broadcast on our ministry's nationwide television program of my message about Pokemon, I was deluged with mail. Much of it was from children and youth. I want to share one such letter here and then show how unbalanced is the reasoning of some of our nation's children.

Dear Phil Arms,

I am fifteen years old, a white male, and very angry over how you criticize Pokemon. I used to play Pokemon until I got too old for it. I now play Dungeons & Dragons. I play it every week with my friends. You probably think we are a bunch of Satanists. Nope! We're all Catholics and Baptists. Try getting a life and quit worrying over a cartoon and a game made in Japan. I can't believe God cares about a game. Have you ever played D & D? You have to be smart. Yes, you do have to kill, but only every once in awhile.

— *Angry in Iowa*

My response to *"Angry in Iowa"* is printed below:

Dear Angry,

Thank you for writing to me and for watching our program. I am sorry you are angry over the facts that I conveyed about Pokemon.

It has been my experience that many people get angry when they are confronted with truths that they do not want to hear. However, your own words and experience have once again proven my point that Pokemon is but an introductory course to even more sinister and demonic games such as D&D.

No, I do not believe that you and your friends are intentionally out worshipping Satan. I do, however, believe that you are walking in great spiritual darkness and have been seduced into believing that your occultic games will have no consequences in your life.

I am here to tell you, Angry, that God has a glorious plan for your life, but in order to experience it you must forsake your involvement with the evil spirits and demonic activities that are so much a part of your recreational habits.

Please be advised that while you and your friends may indeed be good church members, that that is not enough. In order to be a true Christian and to have eternal life, you must enter into a personal relationship with the Lord Jesus Christ. You do this by admitting to God that you are a sinner and that you believe Christ, God's only Son, died on a cross to pay for your sins. Then, by a simple act of faith you must turn your life over to Him, asking Him into your heart. God promises to accept you as you turn all you are over to Him. Then, as you receive His new life you will discover that you no longer want to fellowship and play with the powers of darkness. You will begin to see the evil character of D & D and Pokemon and other such activities.

And, Angry, I do have a life. I found out that true life is only found in Christ who said, "I am the way, the truth, and the life" (John 14:6).

I am not "worried" as you called it, over Pokemon. I am deeply burdened for all the children and young people across the land who are becoming involved through ignorance in the occult and New Age by participating in Pokemon and reading books like the Harry Potter series.

And yes, Angry, God does care about the games we play. Unfortunately, the games we play often parallel our real life experiences. In fact, God cares about everything His people get involved in, and He has laid down clear guidelines in His Word in order to protect us from satanic deception.

No, I have never played D & D, nor do I have to stick my head in a hot oven to know that it will bake my brain.

You say, "You have to be smart to play D & D." I don't think you have to be smart, Angry. I think you need to be deceived and to win such a game is impossible. Even if you win a battle, you lose the war being waged for your very soul.

Your thinking is already showing the signs of moral deterioration. You say you have to "kill, but only every once in awhile." I ask you, Angry, how much killing, how many murders, be they in the heart or in reality, does it take to make a wrong?

I suggest to you, Angry, that you seek the Lord Jesus. Ask God to show you the truth about D & D and to lead you to His Truth.

— In Him, Phil Arms

True Warfare

As parents take a careful look at the facts related to Pokemon and many other popular children's games, books, and programs, many of them will recognize the potential dangers that these activities pose for their children.

Parents need to instruct their children in truths about true spiritual warfare. For true Christians, real life can and should be far more exciting than any fantasy role-playing games children could ever play. In the Christian life there is a great and continual battle going on in which each of us, as well as our children, are involved.

Christians, adults or children, do not need to live in a fantasy world in regard to spiritual warfare. In fact, if anyone really wants to go to war, I encourage them to become a Christian. In the Christian life there is a battle raging every minute. It is a battle to which we are called to participate.

God has provided us with great armor for this warfare. The Bible tells us in Ephesians 6:10–11, "Finally, my brethren, be strong in the Lord and in the power of his might. Put on the whole armour of God, that ye may be able to stand against the wiles of the devil."

Paul, the apostle, goes on in this great passage to define the powerful armor that God has made available to the believer as they enter this spiritual warfare. He mentions being wrapped in Truth, having on the Breastplate of Righteousness, feet shod with the preparation of the Gospel of Peace, having hold of the Shield of Faith which quenches the fiery darts of evil, wearing the Helmet of Salvation, and carrying the Sword of the Spirit which is the Word of God (Eph. 6:12–17).

In Second Corinthians 10:4–5 we are told:

> For the weapons of our warfare are not carnal, but mighty through God to the pulling down of strong holds; Casting down imaginations, and every high thing that exalteth itself against the knowledge of God, and bringing into captivity every thought to the obedience of Christ.

Notice is given to those who would be soldiers of the cross that our weapons are intended for a spiritual battlefield where the warfare is intense.

The word "stronghold" in this passage is referring to a fortress. The Bible is teaching that just as an opposing army may be entrenched in a fortress, that our enemy, with his powerful demonic influences can also become entrenched in our thought lives. As the enemy often sets up these strongholds of wrong thinking in the life of a believer, God provides that believer with the power to rout the enemy and tear down these fortresses of wrong thinking. God provides us with His Word which once installed in our hearts and minds will destroy erroneous concepts and other spiritual strongholds in our lives. As believers apply biblical disciplines to their lives, they are able to stop enemy infiltrations into their thinking processes and to bring their thought lives into harmony with the will and Word of God.

To reinforce these dynamic principles of waging war against the enemy, Paul writes in Romans 12:1-2:

> I beseech you therefore, brethren, by the mercies of God, that ye present your bodies a living sacrifice, holy, acceptable unto God, which is your reasonable service. And be not conformed to this world: but, be ye transformed by the renewing of your mind, that ye may prove what is that good, and acceptable, and perfect, will of God.

The principle for spiritual victory given in this passage is identical to that stated in Second Corinthians 10:4-5. First, believers must surrender their bodies, hearts, and minds exclusively to the will and purposes of God. This means that we tolerate no compromise in the things we allow to enter our hearts and minds.

The motivation for the Christian is their desire to experience the continuing glorious transformation that is initiated by the Spirit of God when they are first born again. It clearly states that this transformation begins in the mind. Again, the mind, or the way we think, is where this warfare is waged. Wrong thinking leads to wrong living. As the Bible states, "As a man thinketh in his heart, so is he." Thus the goal of God's Spirit in our life is to conform our thinking with God's thinking. This alone ensures peace, joy, and power for victorious living.

This renewing process is not just a matter of rejecting the negative reinforcement that we are bombarded with on a daily basis by this world's system. It is a process that demands we take the initiative allowing the eternal life-changing truths and principles of the Word of God to dictate and permeate our way of thinking. This demands a twofold discipline. It means we reject participation in activities that build worldly or demonic anti-Christ thoughts into our ways of thinking and it requires us to aggressively seek to fill our minds and hearts with the transforming Word of God.

I share this principle in order to encourage Christian parents to do more than simply stop their children's involvement with questionable children's games and literature. They should also work aggressively to constantly build the principles of God's Word into their children's thought lives. This, of course, is done by filling their lives with Christian truths, friends, and activities, as well as Bible memory work and Bible storytelling. Children enjoy the creative efforts of loving parents and soak up spiritual truths like sponges soak up water.

Fortunately, an increasing number of Christian ministries have recognized the need for Christian-based children's games, books, and activities and are rushing to fill this need. Consequently, more and more products of this nature are appearing on the market.

Proverbs 4:23 instructs, "Keep thy heart with all diligence; for out of it are the issues of life." The responsibility of godly parents is to protect the heart, or way of thinking, of their children until they are able to do so themselves.

I beseech parents to stand guard over what touches the minds and hearts of their children, remembering the old computer adage, "garbage in, garbage out." By the same token, if parents are instilling the Word of God and its transforming truths into their children, they are building a spiritual hedge around the child while at the same time sowing seeds of life into their young hearts that will one day spring forth in a great harvest.

Chapter 11

Trends

The greatest pressure that adults as well as children and young people face today is peer pressure. And the *pressure* to conform to the *herd mentality,* for most people, is almost irresistible. We may refer to it as being politically correct, cool, with it, or fashionable. But, the truth is, New Age concepts, philosophies, and fads are *in,* and the persuasive powers of society press people to tolerate and integrate New Age viewpoints into many areas of their thinking.

Russel Chandler, who is the religion editor for the *Los Angeles Times*, writes, "The New Age movement is probably the most widespread, powerful phenomena affecting our culture today." Many sociologists are convinced that the New Age movement could possibly impact our culture as much as the Renaissance did its culture.

New Agers passionately believe that their movement will bring in a new world order and a Utopian society marked by peace and prosperity for all mankind. This increasingly popular belief system is an endemic characteristic of most of the contemporary children's literature, programs, movies, and games, including Pokemon. This is no coincidence and is very obviously an integral part of the satanic conspiracy. Tragically, parents are being forced to raise their children in a society where they are literally bombarded at every turn with these New Age, occultic, and satanic concepts, teachings, and doctrines that are being condoned, embraced, and practiced, often by people who have no clue that they are doing so.

I recently read a list of statistics that reveal the spiritual-istic impact that the satanic influences of the New Age are having upon our culture. Below is a partial list of these alarming figures.

- 45% of all Americans believe that ghosts exist.
- 31% of all Americans believe in magical powers.
- 28% believe in witchcraft, 24% in black magic, and 20% in voodoo.
- 42% of American adults believe that they have been in contact with the dead.
- Thirty million Americans believe in reincarnation, a key tenet of New Age beliefs.
- 36% of Americans believe astrological reports are scientific.
- 67% of Americans read their horoscopes.
- 67% of American adults believe they have had psychic experiences.
- 14% of Americans believe in the work of channelers and mediums.

The Attraction

The attractive but deadly lure of a book series like Harry Potter and games like Pokemon is their seemingly positive and harmless appearance. The heroes and their goals all seem to be moving toward creating a better world. The not-so-hidden message in their story lines is their claim to be able to answer life's questions and to solve all of our problems without considering the solutions and answers that are clearly given in the Word of God. In fact, the message of these and many other new children's games and entertainment vehicles is diametrically opposed to the message we have in Christianity.

All humanity, Christians included, would like to see an end to poverty, injustice, and inhumanity. The purported goals of the New Agers are laudable. However, the problem is not with

ultimate goals a
reach these goals
that all human go
of the Lord Jesus C
much of today's chil
possible" through on
spiritual enlightenmen
comes god and, therefor
as well as the way to achi

The only absolute truth
liefs, however, is that they a   re a
combination of spiritualistic su   ctrine, and
various Eastern religious philo   nort, the idea that
man should be his own god is as   as the Luciferian rebellion
recorded in Isaiah 14 of the Old Testament. There we read
how Satan, a powerful angelic being, at some point in time,
decided that he wanted to sit upon the Throne of God. He
instigated an angelic rebellion where approximately one-third
of the heavenly angels sided with him in an attempt to over-
throw God. The rebellion was short-lived and resulted in Lucifer, along with his host of fallen angels, being banished from
the presence of God.

Following that incident, the next time we read of Lucifer,
he is in the Garden of Eden where he appeals to Eve. His temptation was simple: "Eve, be your own god. You don't need Jehovah God. Do as you please and choose against God's revealed
will." This third chapter of the book of Genesis, we read how
Eve and, ultimately, Adam gave into the satanic invitation to
try to accomplish God-given goals in a God-forbidden way. All
along, God intended Adam and Eve to be able to be "one with
Him" by choosing to obey and love Him. However, through a
satanic deception, they attempted to take a short cut to divine
ends and it resulted in the fall of the human race.

Today, Satan is still attempting to work his "magic" by

own god, to realize their own
y forbidden supernatural means to
oals. It may be called New Age think-
ardly anything new in the Edenic conspira-
ted man from God and brought upon humanity
beyond imagination. And, yet, this is the lie and life-
that millions of parents in this nation and around the
world are helping to instill in the lives of their children as
they encourage their involvement in the world of Pokemon,
Harry Potter, and other diabolic activities.

Glossary Of Terms

In their dynamic and revealing book *The Seduction of Our Children,* Neil Anderson and Steve Russo have a glossary that defines the terms used by New Agers and another used by Satanists and occultists.

I feel it is most beneficial to include these in this section. I do so because it will assist parents who are seriously involved in what their children are watching and playing to determine if such activities are something they should be concerned about. Hearing or seeing characters demonstrate these characteristics or using these terms will help a parent identify the nature of the game, book, or program in question as New Age, occultic, or satanic.

New Age Terms

Age of Aquarius. Astrologers believe that evolution goes through cycles directly corresponding to the signs of the zodiac, each lasting approximately two thousand years. Advocates of the New Age say we are now moving in the cycle associated with Aquarius. The Aquarian Age will supposedly be characterized by a heightened degree of spiritual or cosmic consciousness.

Akashic Records. Assumed vast reservoir of knowledge.

Some New Agers believe that the event of all human lives have been recorded in the Universal Mind or Memory of Nature in a region of space known as the ether.

Alchemy. Often associated with medieval folklore, this is a chemical science and speculative philosophy designed to transform base metals into gold. It is figuratively used regarding the change of base human nature into the divine.

Altered States. States other than normal waking consciousness, such as daydreaming; sleep-dreaming; hypnotic trance; meditative, mystical, or drug-induced states; or unconscious states.

Ascended Master. A highly evolved individual no longer required to undergo lifetimes on the physical plan in order to achieve spiritual growth.

Aura. An apparent envelope or field of colored radiation said to surround the human body and other animate objects with the color or colors indicating different aspects of physical, psychological, spiritual conditions.

Biofeedback. A technique using instruments to self-monitor normally unconscious involuntary body processes, such as brain waves, heartbeat, and muscle tension. As this information is fed to the individual he can consciously and voluntarily control internal biological functions.

Channeling. A New Age form of mediumship or spiritism. The channeler yields control of his perceptual and cognitive capacities to a spiritual entity with the intent of receiving paranormal information.

Chakras. The seven energy points on the human body, according to New Agers and yogis. Raising the Kundalini through the chakras is the aim of yoga meditation. Enlightenment (*Samadhi*) is achieved when the Kundalini reaches the "crown chakra" at the top of the head.

Clairaudience. The ability to hear mentally without using the ears.

Clairvoyance. The ability to see mentally beyond ordinary time and space without using the eyes. Also called second sight.

Conciousness. Mental awareness of present knowing. New Agers usually refer to consciousness as the awareness of external objects or facts.

Consciousness Revolution. A New Age way of looking at and experiencing life. The primary focus of the new consciousness is to see the universe as God and see God as the universe.

Cosmic Consciousness. A spiritual and mystical perception that all the universe is one. To attain cosmic consciousness is to see the universe as God and see God as the universe.

Crystals. New Age advocates believe that crystals contain incredible healing and energizing powers. Crystals are often touted as being able to restore the flow of energy in the human body.

Dharma. Law, truth, or teaching. Used to express the central teachings of the Hindu and Buddhist religions. Dharma implies that essential truth can be stated about the way things are, and that people should comply with that norm.

Divination. Methods of discovering the personal, human significance of present or future events. The means to obtain insights may include dreams, hunches, involuntary body actions, mediumistic possession, consulting the dead, observing the behavior of animals and birds, tossing coins, casting lots, and reading natural phenomena.

Esoteric. Used to describe knowledge that is possessed or understood by a select few.

ESP *(extra sensory perception)*. The experience of or response to an external event, object, state, or influence without apparent contact through the known senses. ESP may occur without those involved being aware of it.

Gnosticism. The secret doctrines and practices of mysticism whereby a person may come to the enlightenment or realization that he is of the same essence of God or the Absolute. The Greek word *gnosis* means "knowledge." At the heart of Gnostic thought is the idea that revelation of the hidden *gnosis* frees one from the fragmentary and illusory material world and teaches him about the origins of the spiritual world to which the Gnostic belongs by nature.

The Great Invocation. A New Age prayer that has been translated into over eighty languages. The purpose of this prayer is to invoke the presence of the cosmic Christ on earth, thus leading to the oneness and brotherhood of all mankind.

Harmonic Convergence. The assembly of New Age meditators at the same propitious astrological time in different locations to usher in peace on earth and a one-world government.

Hologram. A three-dimensional projection resulting from the interaction of laser beams. Scientists have discovered that the image of an entire hologram can be reproduced from any one of its many component parts. New Agers use the hologram to illustrate the oneness of all reality.

Higher Self. The most spiritual and knowing part of oneself, said to lie beyond ego, day-to-day personality, and personal consciousness. The higher self can be channeled for wisdom and guidance. Variations include the oversoul, the super-consciousness, the atman, the Christ (or Krishna or Buddha) consciousness, and the God within.

Humanism. The philosophy that upholds the primacy of human beings rather than God or any abstract metaphysical system. Humanism holds that man is the measure of all things.

Human Potential Movement. A movement with roots in humanistic philosophy that stresses man's essential goodness and unlimited potential.

Initiation. An occult term generally used in reference to the expansion or transformation of a person's consciousness. An initiate is one whose consciousness has been transformed to perceive inner realities. There are varying degrees of initiation, such as first degree, second degree, etc.

Inner Self. The inner divine nature possessed by human beings. All people are said to possess an inner self, though they many not be aware of it.

Interdependence/Interconnectedness. Used by New Agers to describe the oneness and essential unity of everything in the universe. All reality is viewed as interdependent and interconnected.

Karma. The debt accumulated against the soul as a result of good or bad actions committed during one's life (or lives). If one accumulates good karma, he supposedly will be reincarnated to a less desirable state.

Kirilian. A type of high-voltage photography using a pulsed, high-frequency electrical field and two electrodes between which are placed the object to be photographed and an unexposed film plate. The image captured is purported to be an aura of energy emanating from plants, animals, and humans that changes in accordance with physiological or emotional shifts.

Magic Circle. A ring drawn by occultists to protect them from the spirits and demons they call up by incantations and rituals.

Mantra. A holy word, phrase, or verse in Hindu or Buddhist meditation techniques. A mantra is usually provided to an initiate by a guru who supposedly holds specific insights regarding the needs of his pupils. The vibrations of the mantra are said to lead the meditator into union with the divine source within.

Monism. Literally means one. In a spiritual framework it refers to the classical occult philosophy that all is one; all reality may be reduced to a single unifying principle partaking of the same essence and reality. Monism also relates to the belief that there is no ultimate distinction between the creator and the creation (pantheism).

Mysticism. The belief that God is totally different from anything the human mind can think and must be approached by a mind without content. Spiritual union or direct communion with ultimate reality can be obtained through subjective experience such as intuition or a unifying vision.

New Age Movement. The most common name for the growing penetration of Eastern and occultic mysticism into Western culture. The words New Age refer to the Aquarian Age which occultists believe is dawning, bringing with it an era of enlightenment and peace. Encompassed within the New Age movement are various cults which emphasize mystic experiences.

Nirvana. Literally a blowing out or cooling of the fires of existence. It is the main term in Buddhism for the final release from the cycle of birth and death into bliss.

Numerology. The analysis of hidden prophetic meanings of numbers.

Pantheism. The belief that God and the world are ultimately identical; all is God. Everything that exists constitutes a unity, and this all-inclusive unity is divine. God is equated with the forces and laws of the universe but is not a personal being.

Paradigm Shift. Refers to a shift in world views. The so-called new paradigm (new model or form) is pantheistic (all is God) and monistic (all is one).

Planetization. New Age advocates believe that the various threats facing the human race require a global solution called planetization. It refers to the unifying of the world into a corporate brotherhood.

Poltergeist. German word for a noisy, mischievous, destructive spirit (demon).

Psi. The twenty-third letter of the Greek alphabet. A general New Age term for ESP, psychokinesis, telepathy, clairvoyance, clairaudience, precognition, and other paranormal phenomena that are nonphysical in nature.

Psychic. A medium, "sensitive," or channeler. Also refers to paranormal events that can't be explained by established physical principles.

Psychic Birth. A quickening of spiritual or cosmic consciousness and power. This new consciousness recognizes oneness with God and the universe. Psychic birth is an occult counterpart to the Christian new birth.

Psychokinesis (PK). The power of the mind to influence matter or move objects (see also telekinesis).

Reincarnation. The belief that the soul moves from one bodily existence to another until, usually after many lives, it is released from historical existence and absorbed into the Absolute.

Right Brain Thinking. The right hemisphere of the brain is believed to be the center of intuitive and creative thought (as opposed to the rational nature of the left hemisphere). New Agers have seized on this as a justification to bring right brain learning techniques into the classroom. These techniques include meditation, yoga, and guided imagery.

Séance. A gathering of people seeking communication with deceased loved ones or famous historical figures through a medium.

Self-Realization. A synonym for God-realization. It refers to a personal recognition of one's divinity.

Shaman. A medicine man or witch doctor.

Spirit Guide. A spiritual entity who provides information or guidance often through a medium or channeler. The spirit provides guidance only after the channeler relinquishes his perceptual and cognitive capacities into its control.

Syncretism. The fusion of different forms of belief or practice; the claim that all religions are one and share the same core teachings.

Synergy. The quality of "whole making"; the New Age belief in the cooperation of natural systems to put things together in ever more meaningful patterns.

Third Eye. An imaginary eye in the forehead believed to be the center of psychic vision.

Tantra. A series of Hindu or Buddhist scriptures concerned with special yogic practices for swift attainment of enlightenment; also the practices, techniques, and traditions of these teachings.

Telekinesis. A form of psychokinesis (PK); the apparent movement of stationary objects without the use of known physical forces.

Trance. An altered state of consciousness, induced or spontaneous, that gives access to many ordinarily inhibited capacities of the mind-body system. Trance states are generally self-induced.

Visualization. Also known as guided imagery; refers to mind over matter. Visualization is the attempt to bring about change in the material realm by the power of the mind.

Yoga. Literally, yoking or joining; any system or spiritual discipline by which the practitioner or yogi seeks to condition the self at all levels — physical, psychical, and spiritual. The goal of the Indian religious tradition is a state of well-being, the loss of self-identity, and absorption into the Absolute or Ultimate Being.

Zen. A type of Buddhist thought best known for its emphasis on breaking down the commitment and attachment to the logical and rational ordering of experiences.

Zodiac. The imaginary belt in the heavens that encompasses the apparent paths of the principle planets except Pluto. Divided into twelve constellations or signs based on the assumed dates that the sun enters each of these "houses" or symbols, the zodiac is used for predictions in astrology.

Satanic/Occultic Terms

Black Mass. Held in honor of the Devil on the witches' sabbath. The ritual reverses the Roman Catholic mass, desecrating the objects used in worship. Sometimes the participants drink the blood of an animal during the ceremony. Often a nude woman is stretched out on the altar, and the high priest concludes the ritual by having sex with her.

Book of Shadows. Also called a *grimoire*, this journal is kept either by individual witches or Satanists or by a coven to record the activities of the group and the incantations used.

Chalice. A silver goblet used for blood communions.

Coven. A group of Satanists who gather to perform rites. There are traditionally thirteen members, but with self-styled groups the number varies. A coven is also called a clan.

Curse. Invocation of an oath associated with black magic or sorcery intended to harm or destroy property or opponents.

Druids. A branch of dangerous and powerful Celtic priests from pre-Christian Britain and Gaul who are still active today. They worship the sun and believe in the immortality of the soul and reincarnation. They are also skilled in medicine and astronomy.

Magick. Magic that employs ritual symbols and ceremony, including ceremonial costumes, dramatic invocations to gods, potent incense, and mystic sacraments.

Magic Circle. A circle inscribed on the floor of a temple for ceremonial purposes. Often nine feet in diameter, it is believed to hold magical powers within and protect those involved in the ceremony from evil.

Magister. The male leader of a coven.

Magus. A male witch.

Necromancy. A practice in which the spirits of the dead are summoned to provide omens for discovering secrets of past or future events.

Necrophilia. An act of sexual intercourse with a corpse.

Occult. From the Latin *occultius,* meaning "secret" or "hidden." The occult refers to secret or hidden knowledge available to initiates, to the supernatural, and sometimes to paranormal phenomena and parapsychology.

Ritual. A prescribed form of religious or magical ceremony.

Runes. A northern European alphabet used by occult groups in secret writing. There are several forms of runering.

Santeria. A mingling of African tribal religions and Catholicism established by African slaves brought to the Americas and the Caribbean.

So Mote It Be. Words spoken at the end of an occult ceremony. Similar to "amen" in traditional religious services.

Talisman. A power object, usually an amulet or trinket.

Voodoo. An ancient religion combining sorcery and Catholicism. Those involved are extremely superstitious and are heavily involved in fetishism.

Warlock. Often used for a male witch, but it actually designates a traitor.

Wicca. The pagan end of the witchcraft spectrum.

Witch. A male or female practitioner of any sort of witchcraft.

Witchcraft. A practice of occultic arts, from Wiccan/nature worship to satanic worship.

I think it equally important to insert for the benefit of our readers the following doctrinal statement of Satanists taken from the same book, *The Seduction of Our Children.*

Nine Statements of Satanic Doctrine

1. Satan represents indulgence instead of abstinence.
2. Satan represents vital existence instead of spiritual pipe dreams.

3. Satan represents undefiled wisdom instead of hypocritical self-deceit.

4. Satan represents kindness to those who deserve it instead of love wasted on ingrates.

5. Satan represents vengeance instead of turning the other cheek.

6. Satan represents responsibility to the responsible instead of concern for psychic vampires.

7. Satan represents man as just another animal, sometimes better, more often worse, than those that walk on all fours, who, because of his "divine spiritual and intellectual development," has become the most vicious animal of all.

8. Satan represents all of the so-called sins, as they all lead to physical, mental, or emotional gratification.

9. Satan has been the best friend the church has ever had, as he has kept it in business all these years.

Perhaps these lists of terms as well as this satanic doctrinal statement will be of great value to astute parents who have decided to stay involved in the activities, programs, and books to which their children are attracted.

Again, I say, the discipline required for parents to protect their children from the influences of evil is demanding. However, loving parents who are willing to make such an investment will reap the reward of eternal dividends in the lives of their children.

Chapter 12

A Searching Heart

It has been my experience that many of the critics I hear from, both young and old, are really seeking truth more than they are trying to be critical.

Such was the case of Amber. I received a letter from this girl after my message, "The Truth About Pokemon," was aired over our national television program. I want to print her letter, along with my response. Perhaps it will shed some light on the way that many of America's youth perceive spiritual things. Hopefully, it will also answer some of the probing questions and dispel many of the illusions that so many of America's youth currently have.

Amber wrote:

Dear Phil Arms,

As I listened to your message on how Pokemon can destroy lives, I came to appreciate even more the underlying purposes of the sermon. It seems that the church operates on a simple fear factor. "Get your followers to believe what you say or else they will go to hell. Send God your money and you won't go to hell. Don't be creative. Don't think for yourself. Just be a sheep and sit there and avoid what we say." HA!

Just a side note about witchcraft that you may have overlooked. It existed long before Christianity. It promotes no evil and no harm. "Ye harm none. Do what ye will . . . and any ill will come back on you three-fold."

Thank you for the opportunity to express my opinion. I welcome any response.

Amber

And so I did respond to Amber and below is part of that response.

Dear Amber,

First, let me say "thank you" for watching our program. You are one of a great number of young people who have written me concerning our "Pokemon" broadcast.

However, I would like to take this opportunity to point out a few very wrong conclusions that you have obviously come to.

Contrary to your statement, the Church of the Lord Jesus Christ does not operate on fear. It functions on a premise of Divine and supernatural love.

The Bible teaches us that God has not given us a spirit of fear, but of love, power, and a sound mind (2 Tim. 1:7). It is the love and light of God the Father that dispels the dark, evil confusion of satanic forces in our lives and provokes us to live a life of loving submission to the will of our Lord.

Additionally, our television ministry, missions outreaches, and evangelistic efforts do not exist to simply get people to send money. Because godly people care about the eternal destination of others, they send money so our ministries can exist. This ministry is supported by precious folks from all over America because they love people like you, Amber. These people are burdened for our nation's spiritual welfare and long with all their hearts to share God's Truth with others. Because of their burden, they, without being asked, sacrificially give in order to touch the lives of people that they do not even know with the liberating truths of God's Word.

In fact, Amber, I am enclosing as a gift to you the Pokemon series so that you can hear the messages in their entirety.

And, by the way, Amber, no one escapes hell or receives God's gift of eternal life by doing good deeds, like sending money to ministries. The only way to ensure one's place in heaven is to surrender one's life to the Lord Jesus Christ and make Him the Lord of that life. It is Christ who came, out of love, to die for all of our sins on a cross, and He is our only hope of eternal salvation.

It is in this personal relationship with Him that we discover our purpose in this life and are able to experience God's grace, power, and peace.

I want you to know, Amber, that God loves you and Satan has deceived you.

By the way, you are wrong about witchcraft being around longer than Christianity. I have written books and articles, as well as preached numerous messages, on the origin of witchcraft.

Christianity is not dated from the birth of Christ. Jesus is, has always been, and always will be. In the first chapter of the Gospel of John, Jesus is called The Word. It says of Him in verses 1–5, "In the beginning was the Word, and the Word was with God, and the Word was God. The same was in the beginning with God. All things were made by him; and without him was not anything made that was made. In him was life; and the life was the light of men. And the light shineth in darkness; and the darkness comprehended it not."

You see, Amber, all religions, outside the Christian faith, are mere counterfeits originated by man and Satan as a way of escaping their true obligation to acknowledge God and to be accountable to Him.

While the Wiccan religion which you quote and defend denies the existence of a personal devil, the fact is, he is the true deity behind its inception. He is the Father of Lies and he has lied to you.

You are alive, Amber, so that you can come to know your Creator. You do not exist because Mother Nature formed you out of natural evolutionary processes or because you were recycled through reincarnation.

It is the Wiccan religion that is based on darkness, deceit, death, and fear. Even the Wiccan phrase you wrote me, "Know that any ill will come back on you threefold," is a truth stolen from the Word of God. It says, "You reap what you sow."

Amber, do not let the evil lying spirit of witchcraft keep you from coming to know your true Lord and Savior, Jesus Christ.

Please know that I have asked all of our television viewers and friends to join me in praying for your eyes to be opened to the "glorious truths of the Gospel."

I am enclosing a number of other items and messages that will help you see the deep deception behind the Wiccan religion. Do not send any money for any of these items as they are a gift.

And, please, feel free to call our toll-free number, or to write us with any needs or questions you have.

God bless you and may His Spirit lead you to His Truth.

In Christ, Phil Arms

Observation

The children's programs, activities, and books that present a great spiritual danger to children today, such as Pokemon and the Harry Potter series, will one day no longer be popular with children.

Satanic efforts to corrupt and poison the hearts and minds of our children are always on the cutting edge of contemporary technology and popular trends. Soon the fad of Pokemon and Harry Potter will pass, only to be replaced by new or more appealing traps laid by the Luciferian conspirators. But, parents need not be in the dark. The techniques and satanic fundamentals that are so obvious in current children's attractions will be just as obvious in any future attractions.

As my wife and I discussed the best way to help parents recognize future assaults through coming children's games and literature she said, "The occult is the occult is the occult. Different names, different games, but all are one and the same." And she is quite right. Satan and his cohorts may try to camouflage the true nature of their intended agents of influence, but informed and discerning parents can always be prepared to see through the demonic mask.

Telling Signs

I want to give parents a list of themes and items to watch for in the programming, books, and games they are considering for their children. These "marks" are often good indications that occultic, New Age, or satanic influences can be found in that particular subject matter. Some of these are more obvious indications of evil than others, but parents should consider all of them as fingerprints of satanic influences.

I have compiled the following list from numerous sources, but I am indebted to my friend, author David Benoit and his fantastic book, *Who's Watching the Playpen?*, for much of it.

When the following themes and characteristics are noticed by parents in their children's entertainment they should move to intervene.

1. **Violence.** Most of the violence depicted in today's children's games and stories is far beyond the slapstick variety of violence in past children's attractions. Parents should be concerned when characters are pictured (or told about) being blown to pieces, poisoned, maimed, butchered, or killed with bloody fury.

2. **Evolution** (or mutated characters). Parents should remember that the anti-Christian, humanistic theory of evolution is still one of the most popular and often used themes promoted on children's television and in their stories and games.

The promotion of this unscientific, antiquated concept through children's programs is no accident. Occultists and New Agers know that they must be able to convince children that there is no God who created the universe if they are to succeed in their effort to convert these young minds to their hellish doctrine. One of the most popular approaches to this goal is by the introduction of the concept of mutations.

Pokemon, Harry Potter, and most other children's games and books feature characters who evolved into their current state. Often these characters are superheroes like the Teenage Mutant Ninja Turtles who evolved into mutations with supernatural powers.

3. **Goddess Worship**. It should be noted that the Wiccan religion (the religion of witchcraft) has as their deities Mother Earth and the Great Green Goddess. The truth is, however, the true god behind the witches' religion, unbeknownst to them, is Satan, the Author of Lies.

David Benoit, in his powerful book *Who's Watching the Playpen?* writes, "Today, feminists and witches are attacking the fact that God is a male gender. There is a new Bible on the market that refers to 'His/Her' or 'Our Mother/Father which art in heaven.'"

Mainline denominations are accepting Sophia as a substitute of Jesus Christ. (Examples of this are found in "Captain Planet.")

4. **Supernatural powers and entities and personalities**. Listed below are various references to these themes that should alert any concerned parent:

a. **Elements**. Witchcraft relies heavily upon interaction with earth, wind, fire, water, a

b. **Wizards and the use of magic**. Harry Pot mon feature the constant dependency upon wizardry and their magical powers.

c. **Spirits**. Quite often spirits are pictured as being benevolent and even helpful entities. Parents must remember that when children are being encouraged to invite a spirit guide to enter their lives they are literally inviting demons into their world.

d. **Power symbols**. The use of crystals, elements, and things, such as magic wands, all of which are promoted by the children's activities we have mentioned are occultic and dangerous.

e. **Mediation**. The subtle promotion of this New Age concept fill children's programs, games, and literature.

f. **Reincarnation**. The teaching of reincarnation via children's activities is one of the most common occurrences that observant parents will discover. This New Age concept was heavily relied upon in programs like *The Lion King, Casper,* and *Pocahontas.*

g. **Telepathic and psychic abilities**. This refers to the ability to communicate with others by the use of one's mental powers. Often characters in the games and stories are featured as sending messages by the act of sheer will-power exerted upon the mind.

h. **Visualization**. This New Age and occult concept teaches that reality can be created by focused meditation.

These are but a few of the occultic/New Age themes that fill most of today's children's entertainment.

When parents recognize any of these themes or the use of any of these occultic techniques utilized in their children's entertainment, they should act as warning signs. Children

...iould be taught, as we have already pointed out, to recognize the use of these evil concepts and to report such occurrences to their parent.

I reiterate, parents should not only stop their children from involvement with evil, but they should always be prepared to steer their children toward spiritually healthy and edifying activities. Additionally, parents must be very careful not to instill fear into their child when attempting to educate them about evil. This can be avoided by the balanced emphasis a parent places on training their children in the memorization of Scripture.

We have the promises from God which ensures us that the Word of God will not return void, but will accomplish that for which it is sent. Of great comfort to every parent is the wonderful assurance we have from the Father that as we protect, nurture, and train our children in the ways of God, when they become adults they will not forsake the glorious truths that we have imparted to them.

The Bible says, "Train up a child in the way he should go: and when he is old, he will not depart from it" (Prov. 22:6)

A Final Word

As a parent of three children, one of them still nine years old, I must tell you that the vigilance, dedication, and sheer willpower necessary to successfully protect a child from the many satanic traps laid to ruin their lives is not an easy task. And, yet, this is what God requires of Christian parents. He provides the strength, the wisdom, and the weaponry we need as His people to fight this war for the destiny of our children.

It takes absolute commitment, but far beyond commitment, it demands that a parent first know the Lord Jesus Christ as their personal Lord and Savior.

For those parents who refuse His love, His mercy, and His grace, I can offer no hope that their children will escape the satanic snares that are craftily laid before them. But, for those fathers and mothers who lay claim to the Kingdom of God because of their abiding relationship with Christ, there is for them a peace that passes all understanding that their precious children will not only escape the best-laid plans of hell to destroy their young lives, but that indeed their children will one day become mighty warriors for the King of Kings. Then, as they have little ones born into their own families, they as loving parents will pass on to their children the torch that lights our dark world with the precious truths of the Word of God.

Know therefore that the Lord thy God, he is God, the faithful God, who keepeth covenant and mercy with them who love him and keep his commandments to a thousand generations.
— Deuteronomy 7:9

Other Resources by Phil Arms

Books

Wet Flies Can't Fly . . . or The Keys to the Victorious Christian Life

The Winner in You

Promise Keepers: Another Trojan Horse

Co-Authored by Phil Arms

The Triumphant Return of Christ

Earth's Final Days

Piercing the Future

Videos/Audio Tapes

How to Enrich Your Family

Magic and Demons

A Date with the Devil (on Christian dating)

Building a Spiritual Hedge

Prophecy: The Last Generation

X-Files and the Bible: The UFO Craze, Fact or Fiction?

The Antichrist and His Strategy for America

World War III

To receive a free full-color resource catalog, call

1-800-829-9673

or write

Phil Arms Ministries

P.O. Box 299

Thompsons, TX 77481

About the Author

Phil Arms is a nationally known pastor-evangelist whose radio and television ministries have touched the lives of millions. He has authored or co-authored seven other books ranging on topics from prophecy to victorious Christian living. He is currently a featured speaker at Bible conferences and evangelistic campaigns across America. Phil and Suzanne Arms live in Houston, Texas, with their daughter Linsdsay and son Philip.

For interviews or to discuss the possibility of hosting Phil Arms in your area, call 1-800-829-9673, or write Phil Arms Ministries, P.O. Box 299, Thompsons, TX 77481.